Kids' Quilts
in a
Weekend®

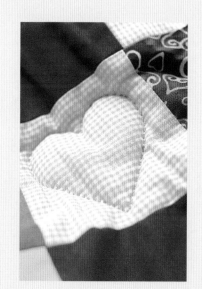

Kids' Quilts in a Weekend®

20 colourful projects suitable
for babies to 10-year-olds

Elizabeth Keevill

hamlyn

First published in Great Britain in 2004 by
Hamlyn, a division of Octopus Publishing Group Ltd
2–4 Heron Quays, London E14 4JP

First published in paperback in 2006

ISBN-13: 978-0-600-61489-0
ISBN-10: 0-600-61489-1

A CIP catalogue record for this book is
available from the British Library

Printed and bound in China

10 9 8 7 6 5 4 3 2 1

Contents

Introduction 6

Lazy Weekend 9

Lively Weekend 39

Busy Weekend 73

Materials, Equipment
& Techniques 105

Index 142
Acknowledgements 144

Introduction

Unlike many favourite toys that are often just a passing fad, a quilt is a gift that a child will treasure for years. Once outgrown as a bed cover, it can be displayed as a wall hanging or may be handed on to the next generation as an heirloom. Quilt-making has a reputation for being a time-consuming craft, involving many hours of close work and endless patience. Today, however, there are modern tools, materials and time-saving tips, which make it possible to produce a quilt in a relatively short space of time.

How to use this book

Kids' Quilts in a Weekend® is divided into four sections. The first contains the least complex projects, which can be made up easily in a weekend. The projects in the second section require more effort to complete in a weekend and need a slightly wider range of skills. Section three contains projects for which some advance preparation is necessary as well as greater skill. The fourth section offers information on the materials, equipment, skills and techniques that you will need to complete the projects, even if starting from scratch. Once you have chosen a project, read through the instructions carefully from start to finish to make sure you understand the work involved. Specific materials and equipment are listed and followed by a step-by-step description of how the quilt is assembled.

Working with fabric

Sewing involves repeated handling of the fabric and, unless you take care, material can become grimy very quickly. Wash your hands before you start and never eat while you are working. Cut fabric in batches, or cut out just enough for one session, and store in clear plastic bags. Keep your work in progress clean by storing the whole project – including templates or patterns – in a large plastic bag. Make sure you keep any patchwork pieces flat once they are cut out: ironing them after cutting can cause distortion and may lead to inaccuracies in piecing.

All fabric quantities take into account the width of the fabric and allow a little extra for error. If, however, you are using up scraps of fabric, you may be able to get away with using less.

To avoid wastage, cut the pieces from your fabric as economically as possible: cutting guides have been provided for a number of projects.

All measurements are given in metric with imperial conversions. Where accuracy is vital, the conversions are exact. Otherwise the amounts have been rounded up or down and will not be direct equivalents. For this reason, use either metric or imperial, but do not mix the two.

Safety notes

When making articles for children and babies, it is essential that the materials you use are safe and that you construct the object carefully so as to avoid accidents. In particular:

Make sure the object is carefully sewn and securely finished off so that stuffing, filling and wadding cannot come out, which could cause choking.

Never have quilts dry-cleaned: fumes from the cleaning fluid can remain in the article, which could result in death if the quilt were used on a child's bed.

Scissors, seam rippers, craft knives, needles, pins and rotary cutters can all be very dangerous to small children. Keep all your equipment in a safe place, out of the reach of children, while you are working, and once you have finished a project.

Take note of any age restrictions given in the project. Small items such as buttons, beads and pompoms can be chewed off and must not be used on quilts for children under three years.

Babies can overheat if their bedding is too warm and this may be a contributory factor to cot death, or Sudden Infant Death Syndrome (SIDS). Use only very lightweight quilts on a baby's cot, and only in cooler weather.

Lazy Weekend

In a short space of time you can make a beautiful gift that will be treasured for many years to come.

Here are six basic projects that demonstrate how striking colours and stunning fabrics can be used to make something very simple look truly outstanding. Each project can be completed in a weekend following the simple instructions, once you have assembled the necessary materials and equipment.

Quick & Easy Snuggle Quilt

The finished size of the comforter is approximately 180 x 115cm (71 x 45in), which makes it suitable as a topper for a single bed or a sofa cuddle quilt. The exact size of your finished comforter will depend on the pattern of your chosen fabric and its width.

Filled with high-loft polyester wadding for maximum warmth and cosiness, this easy-to-make comforter will become your child's firm favourite for snuggling on the sofa, as a bed topper or for sleepovers with friends. The fabric is already printed with a patchwork-effect pattern, which allows you to produce a complex-looking quilt in the minimum of time. Choose a simpler, smaller-scale or plain fabric for the backing, in colours that coordinate with the top fabric – we have used pink gingham.

✂ you will need

Fabric quantities assume a width of at least 140cm (55in)
Seam allowance: 1.5cm (⅝in)

- 200cm (79in) patchwork-effect or large-check fabric for the quilt top (exact quantities will depend on the pattern)

- 200cm (79in) pink gingham for the backing (exact quantities will depend on the pattern)

- 190 x 120cm (75 x 47in), 55g (2oz) or 115g (4oz) polyester wadding (batting) (the exact size will depend on your choice of fabric and the size of the quilt. As a rule, your piece of wadding should be at least the same size as the finished quilt.)

- four bulldog clips, strong clothes pegs or large safety pins for 'bagging out'

- white sewing thread

- pink hand-quilting thread

- see also basic equipment (page 108)

to make the quilt

1 Before you cut your fabric, decide on the exact size of your quilt, taking into account the design of the fabric and ensuring you include complete pattern repeats. Add 3cm (1¼in) both to the width and the length to allow for 1.5cm (⅝in) seams all round and cut a rectangle of fabric to form the top of the quilt (✂ 1). Our quilt top is made from a piece of fabric 183 x 118cm (72 x 46½in).

2 Using the quilt top as your template, cut a rectangle from the pink gingham for the quilt backing.

3 'Bag out' the quilt and insert the wadding following the instructions on page 120.

4 Pin-baste the quilt all over, avoiding the areas where you will be quilting, following the instructions on page 112.

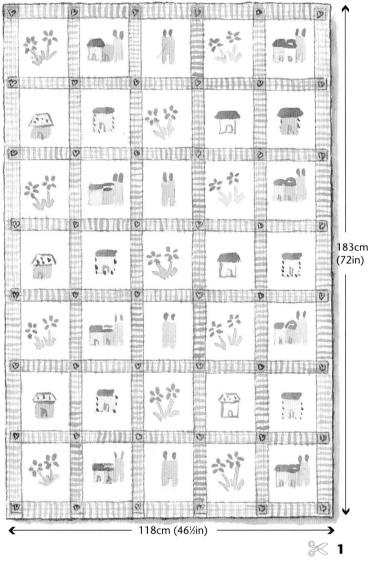

183cm (72in)

118cm (46½in)

✂ 1

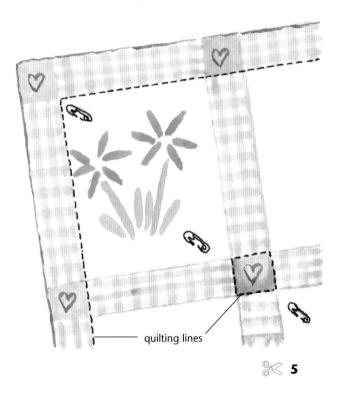

quilting lines

✂ 5

5 Using pink quilting thread, hand-quilt all round the comforter to form a border about 5cm (2in) from the outer edge. The exact distance will depend on the design of your fabric (✂ 5).

6 Hand-quilt around the central squares in the same way.

Quilting by hand

While not as fast as quilting by machine, this technique has a distinctive quality and, on a quilt this size, does not take long. Hand-quilting is also the better choice for thick quilts such as this one (if you have used 115g (4oz) wadding), which can be tricky to manoeuvre on a machine. If you have used 55g (2oz) wadding you may prefer to machine-quilt (see page 112). If you find it tricky to sew around the central squares by machine, try sewing two sides at a time, cutting the thread and then rotating the quilt by 90 degrees so you can sew the other two sides from the same angle.

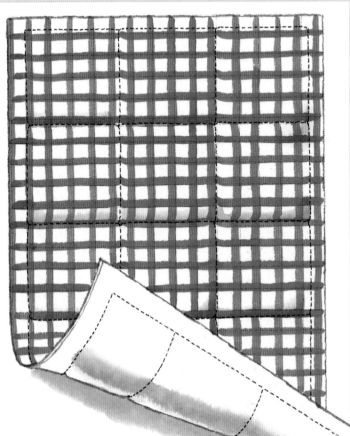

Alternatives

Any patchwork-style fabric is suitable for this project and a large-check fabric would do equally well. The design on the fabric not only provides the guide for the size of the quilt but also a guide for the quilting; the exact pattern of the quilting will therefore vary according to your fabric. In our design, we have hand-quilted around the central squares. You may be able to copy this idea, or a further option is to 'tie' the central panel of the comforter instead of, or in addition to, quilting it by hand (see page 113).

Soft & Tufty Comforter

The finished size of the quilt is approximately 160 x 115cm (63 x 45in). It can be used as a tucked-in cot quilt or as a single-bed topper. Alternatively you could, if you wish, make the quilt larger, in which case you will need to use wider fabric or sheeting or join lengths of fabric together.

This eye-catching and quick-to-make comforter is made from single pieces of 'shot' handwoven fabric with a lively contrasting print for the binding, which was the source of inspiration for the colour scheme. Rather than having stitched quilting, this quilt is tied. The technique is much quicker than sewn quilting and is particularly effective when used in conjunction with high-loft polyester wadding, resulting in a plump, dimpled effect. Futon-style tufts create an interesting random pattern.

✂ you will need

Fabric quantities assume a width of at least 115cm (45in)
Seam allowance 1.5cm (⅝in)

- 160cm (63in) turquoise fabric for the quilt top

- 160cm (63in) orange fabric for the backing

- 80cm (32in) patterned fabric for binding strips

- 165 x 120cm (65 x 47in) good-quality 115g (4oz) bonded polyester wadding (batting)

- light-blue sewing thread

- two skeins primrose-yellow soft embroidery thread

- crewel needle (embroidery needle) with a large eye

- see also basic equipment (page 108)

Note To avoid the danger of choking, do not make the tufts too long, particularly for younger children. Ensure they are tightly and securely knotted and check regularly for fraying or loosening of the threads.

to make the comforter

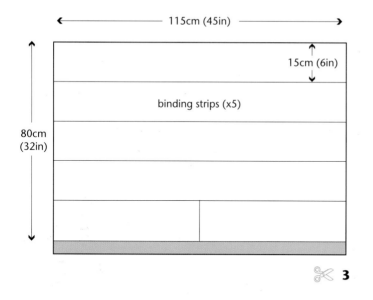

115cm (45in)

15cm (6in)

binding strips (x5)

80cm
(32in)

3

1 Cut a 150 x 106cm (59 x 41¾in) rectangle from the turquoise fabric. Using this as a template, cut the orange backing fabric 4.5cm (1¾in) larger all round than the turquoise fabric. The orange fabric will therefore measure 159 x 115cm (62½ x 45in). Use the orange fabric as a template to cut the wadding to the same size.

2 Lay the orange fabric on the floor, wrong side up (if applicable), spreading it out carefully. Lay the wadding on top, smoothing out any wrinkles, and centre the turquoise fabric on top of the wadding. You should have an even border of wadding visible all round. With the turquoise fabric uppermost, pin-baste the three layers together following the instructions on page 112.

3 Cut five binding strips 15cm (6in) deep from the whole width of the patterned fabric (✄ 1). Cut one of the binding strips in half and join each half to another strip, end-to-end, so that you have two short strips and two long ones. Prepare each strip following the instructions on page 121.

4 Using light-blue sewing thread, bind the edges of the quilt beginning with the short ends, following the instructions on page 122.

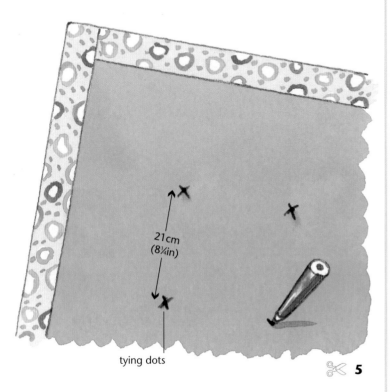

21cm
(8¼in)

tying dots

✄ 5

5 With the turquoise fabric uppermost, mark tying dots on the surface of the quilt, approximately 21cm (8¼in) apart (✄ 5).

6 Cut 12 pieces of primrose-yellow soft embroidery thread 100cm (39in) long and follow the instructions on page 113 to 'tie' the quilt. Work in horizontal rows and use reef knots. Use sharp scissors to trim the tufts to 1.5cm (⅝in) for children under three years old and up to 5cm (2in) for older children.

Alternatives

You can choose any printed or patterned fabric for the binding and select plain, coordinating colours for the front and back panels. Instead of using one colour of embroidery thread you could use multicoloured thread or fine embroidery ribbon. The quilt can be buttoned (see page 113) or a row of buttons could be added between each row of ties. However, buttons are not suitable for children under three years old.

Powder-coloured Diamonds

Cheerful and summery, this quilt has a bright, geometrical design that is likely to appeal to older children. Large squares are cut from powder-coloured fabrics and arranged diagonally following a traditional arrangement known as 'on point'. The vertical and horizontal quilting lines break up the large diamonds into smaller triangular shapes, while the patterned fabrics add further interest.

The finished size of the quilt is approximately 202 x 148cm (79½ x 58in) making it suitable for use on a standard single bed.

✂ you will need

Fabric quantities assume a fabric width of at least 150cm (59in) unless stated otherwise*. Seam allowance 1.5cm (⅝in)

- 70cm (28in) light-blue fabric with darker dots

- 70cm (28in) light-pink fabric with darker dots

- 70cm (28in) dark-pink fabric

- 70cm (28in) purple-blue fabric

- 70cm (28in) light-blue fabric

- 50cm (20in) light-green fabric

- 50cm (20in) mid-blue fabric

- 50cm (20in) turquoise fabric

- 30cm (12in) jade fabric

- 210cm (83in) blue fabric for backing or 150cm (59in) of wide-width* sheeting (at least 210cm (83in) wide)

- 210 x 150cm (83 x 59in) 55g (2oz) polyester wadding (batting)

- light-blue sewing thread

- invisible quilting thread

- see also basic equipment (page 108)

- thin card for the templates, cut as follows:
  23cm (9in) square
  20cm (7¾in) square

to make the quilt

1 From the light-blue fabric with darker dots cut seven binding strips 11cm (4⅜in) deep by 110cm (59in) wide from across the width of the fabric, then from the remainder of the fabric cut 12 squares using the 23cm (9in) template. Still with the 23cm (9in) template cut the following squares:
- light-pink fabric with darker dots (twelve)
- dark-pink fabric (twelve)
- purple-blue fabric (twelve)
- light-blue fabric (nine)
- light-green fabric (eight)
- mid-blue fabric (eight)
- turquoise fabric (six)
- jade fabric (four)

2 Lay the squares out on the floor in the correct order (✂ 2). Starting at the top left-hand corner, join the squares in each diagonal row taking 1.5cm (⅝in) seams and using a light-blue sewing thread (see instructions on page 110). For accuracy, draw seam lines on the back using the 20cm (7¾in) square and a vanishing marker. Machine-sew, then press the seams open and mark each row with its number (see page 110).

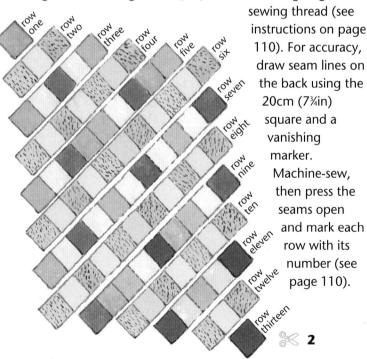

✂ **2**

3 Lay out the rows and pin to each other in the correct order, ensuring that you stagger the beginning of each row and that the seams align from row to row (see page 111). Press the seams open.

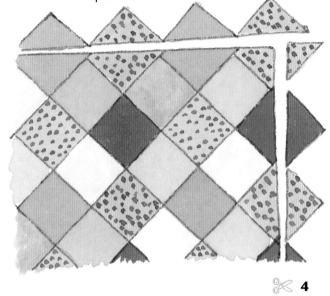

✂ **4**

4 Square off the quilt top by drawing a line 1.5cm (⅝in) further out than an imaginary line that links the points of the diamonds all round the edge of the quilt (✂ 4). Cut along this line to form a rectangular quilt top. The extra 1.5cm (⅝in) is to create a seam allowance around the edge of the quilt for the binding stage.

5 Use the quilt top as a template to cut the blue backing fabric 3cm (1¼in) larger all round. Cut the wadding to the same size as the backing. Lay the backing fabric on the floor, wrong side up (if applicable), spreading it out carefully. Lay the wadding on top, smoothing out any wrinkles, and centre the quilt top on the wadding. You should have an even border of wadding visible all round. With the quilt top uppermost, pin-baste the three layers together following the instructions on page 112.

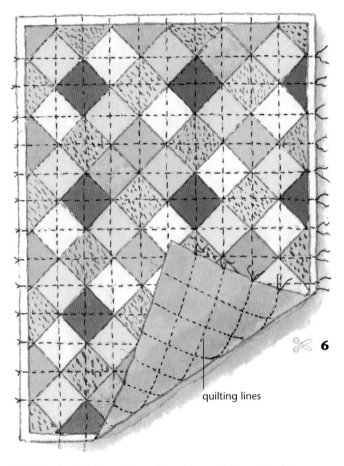

quilting lines

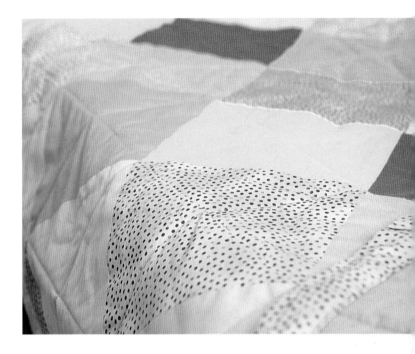

✂ **6**

6 Using invisible quilting thread, quilt in vertical lines, linking the points of the diamonds (✂ 6). Sew in one direction – from top to bottom only – otherwise the quilt will distort. You will need to roll up the right-hand side of the quilt to sew the left-hand lines (see page 113). When you have quilted all the vertical lines, quilt the horizontal lines. To avoid puckering and bunching because you are sewing on the bias (across the weave of the fabric), you will need to stretch the fabric gently at right angles to the quilting line as you go. Place your hands on the fabric on either side of the needle and smooth your hands across the fabric, away from the needle, as you sew.

7 Join two pairs of the binding strips, end-to-end, to form two long strips. Cut one of the remaining binding strips in half and join each half to each of the two other remaining strips in the same way. You will now have two short and two long strips. Prepare each strip following the instructions on page 121.

8 Using light-blue sewing thread, bind the edges of the quilt beginning with the long sides, following the instructions on page 122.

Alternatives
If you have used good-quality bonded polyester wadding you can tie the quilt in the centre of each diamond with a red soft embroidery cotton tie (see page 113). A small cross-stitch where the diamonds intersect would also help to hold the layers in place.

Undersea Laundry Bag

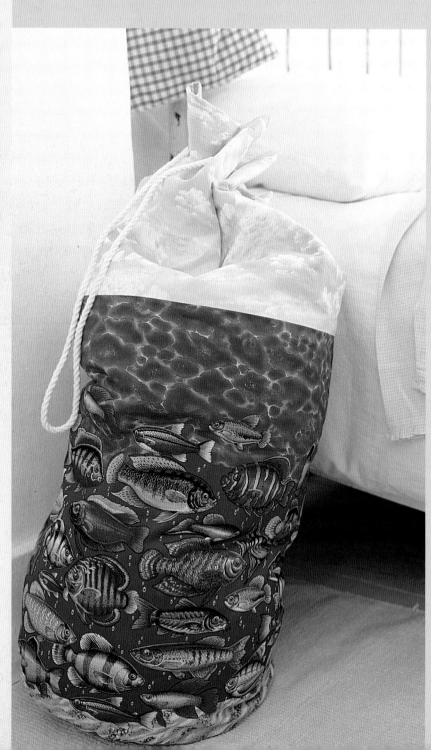

This striking laundry bag is bound to encourage kids to put their dirty clothes away tidily rather than leaving them strewn on the bedroom floor. Relying on a wonderful mixture of novelty fabrics for its effect, the bag has eyelets and rope around the top, which fit with the nautical theme. Pre-wash the fabrics and bond the fish on carefully and you should be able to machine-wash the bag to keep it sweet and fresh.

The finished size of the bag is approximately 90 x 52cm (35½ x 20½in) but you can make it larger or smaller to suit a multitude of purposes.

✂ you will need

Fabric quantities assume a width of at least 110cm (43in) unless stated otherwise*
Seam allowance 1.5cm (⅝in)

- 70cm (28in) sand-and-pebble print fabric

- 40cm (16in) fish-print fabric

- 60cm (24in) sky-print fabric

- 30cm (12in) sea-print fabric

- 120cm (47in) white or light-blue fabric to line the bag (sheeting is fine)

- 40cm (16in) firm iron-on interfacing, 91cm (36in) wide*

- 120cm (47in) fusible webbing, 46cm (18in) wide*

- light-blue, white and sand-coloured sewing threads

- 105cm (41in) light-weight iron-on wadding (batting), 89cm (35in) wide*

- 20cm (8in) cm soft iron-on interfacing, 91cm (36in) wide*

- ten x 1.4mm (½in) eyelets and fixing tool

- 150cm (59in) cotton or nylon rope, max. 1cm or (⅜in) diameter (ask for the ends of the rope to be sealed)

- see also basic equipment (page 108)

- paper for the templates, cut as follows: 36.5cm (14⅜in) diameter circle 33.5cm (13³⁄₁₆in) diameter circle

Note As the bag has rope threaded in it, it should not be given to children under three years old or left within their reach.

to make the laundry bag

1 With the sand-and-pebble fabric spread out widthways, cut a 36.5cm (14⅜in) diameter circle from the top corner and trim the remaining fabric across the width to make a rectangle measuring 110 x 33.5 cm (43 x 13³⁄₁₆in). Cut two 33.5cm (13³⁄₁₆in) diameter circles from the firm interfacing. Iron one to the centre of the wrong side of the fabric circle you have just cut and reserve the other one for later.

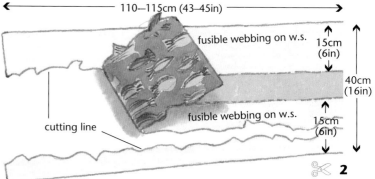

110–115cm (43–45in)

fusible webbing on w.s.

15cm (6in)

40cm (16in)

15cm (6in)

cutting line

fusible webbing on w.s.

✂ **2**

2 Cut two strips of fusible webbing 15cm (6in) deep and same width as the fish fabric. Press the webbing to the top and bottom edges of the wrong side of the fish fabric, according to the webbing manufacturer's instructions. Following the shapes of the fish and keeping as near as possible to the centre line of each webbing section, cut around the fish using small scissors (✂ 2). This should give you a shaped edge, top and bottom. Cut out any complete fish shapes from the fabric remnants and put to one side.

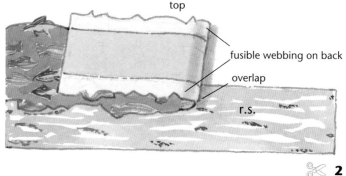

top

fusible webbing on back

overlap

r.s.

✂ **2**

3 Lay the sand-and-pebble fabric out widthways, right side up. Place the fish fabric panel above it, right side up, with the fish the correct way up. Slide the fish fabric over the sand fabric until the top edge of the fusible webbing on the lower part of the fish fabric lines up exactly with the top edge of the sand fabric (✂ 3). (You can place pins at the edge of the webbing to help you overlap the fabrics accurately.) Fuse the fabrics together following the manufacturer's instructions.

4 Lay the sea fabric out widthways, right side up. Place the top edge of the fish fabric over the bottom edge of the sea fabric and, as before, position the area of fusible webbing so the edge of the sea fabric coincides with the edge of the webbing. Fuse together.

5 Bond the reserved cut-out fish the correct way up onto the sea and sand-and-pebble areas.

6 The total height of the three pieces of bonded fabric should be approximately 56cm (22in). If it is much more than this, trim the sea and sand fabrics carefully in a straight line at a right angle to the selvage.

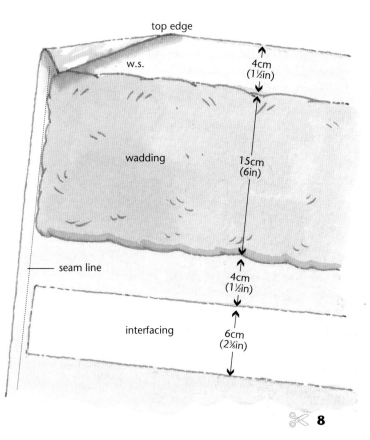

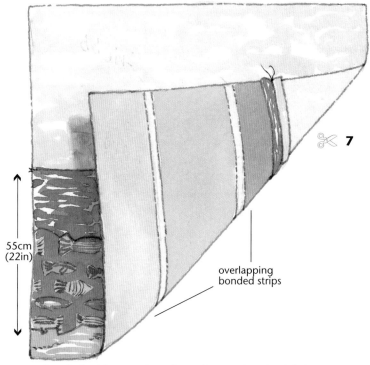

7 Using light-blue sewing thread, sew the sky fabric to the top edge of the sea fabric, taking a 1.5cm (⅝in) seam (✂ 7). Press the seam open.

8 Cut a 15cm (6in) strip off one long edge of the iron-on wadding. Put the rest of the wadding to one side. Working on the wrong side of the sky fabric, position the top edge of this strip 4cm (1½in) down from the top edge of the sky fabric, starting and finishing just short of the seam lines (✂ 8). Iron in place following the manufacturer's instructions. From the whole width of the soft iron-on interfacing, cut two 6cm (2⅜in) deep strips. Place the strips of interfacing end-to-end across the width of the fabric, leaving a 4cm (1½in) gap below the wadding strip, and starting just short of the left-hand seam line (✂ 8). You will need to trim the end of the second piece just short of the right-hand seam line. Iron in place following the manufacturer's instructions.

9 To make the bag, fold the fabric in half lengthways, right sides together, and pin the short edges to form a tube, matching up the sea/sky seams. Machine-stitch the seams using light-blue sewing thread and press them open, but leave the tube inside out.

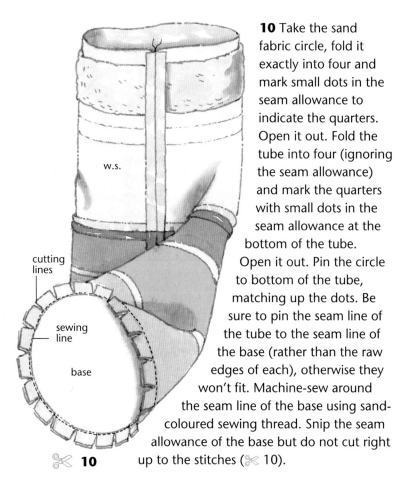

w.s.

cutting lines

sewing line

base

✂ **10**

10 Take the sand fabric circle, fold it exactly into four and mark small dots in the seam allowance to indicate the quarters. Open it out. Fold the tube into four (ignoring the seam allowance) and mark the quarters with small dots in the seam allowance at the bottom of the tube. Open it out. Pin the circle to bottom of the tube, matching up the dots. Be sure to pin the seam line of the tube to the seam line of the base (rather than the raw edges of each), otherwise they won't fit. Machine-sew around the seam line of the base using sand-coloured sewing thread. Snip the seam allowance of the base but do not cut right up to the stitches (✂ 10).

11 Cut a rectangle of lining fabric 108 x 77cm (42½ x 30¼in). Lay the lining fabric out flat and centre the rest of the wadding on it. There should be a narrow margin of fabric extending all round the edge. Iron the wadding onto the fabric, following the manufacturer's instructions.

12 Pin the longer sides of the lining fabric together to form a tube and sew along the seam, leaving a 20cm (8in) gap in the middle. Use light-blue or white sewing thread, depending on the colour of the lining fabric. Press the seam open. Cut a 36.5cm (14⅜in) circle of lining fabric and centre the reserved 33.5cm (13³⁄₁₆in) diameter circle of firm interfacing on the wrong side. Iron in place following the manufacturer's instructions. Sew the circle to one end of the lining tube, following the instructions in step 10.

13 Turn the lining inside out, so that the raw edges are on the inside. With the outer bag also turned inside out, place the lining bag inside the outer bag. The right sides of both bags should be together. Line up the side seams and pin the two bags together along the top edge, with raw edges level. The base of the lining will be higher than the base of the outer bag (✂ 13). Machine-sew along the seam line at the top of the bags using light-blue sewing thread.

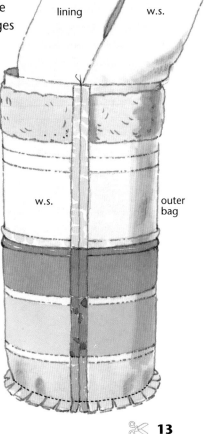

lining w.s.

w.s. outer bag

✂ **13**

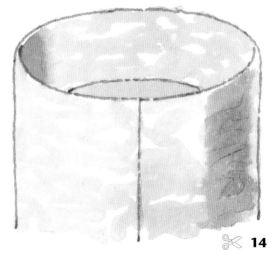

✂ **14**

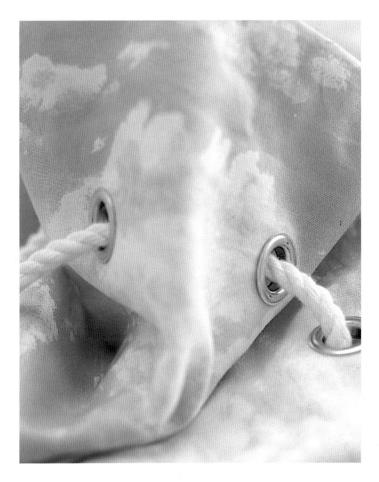

14 Pull the outer bag out through the opening in the lining and turn both parts right sides out. Oversew (see page 117) or machine-stitch (by pinching the edges together) the gap in the lining. Use light-blue or white sewing thread depending on the colour of the lining fabric. Push the lining bag down inside the outer bag so the base circles lie on top of each other – now there should be about 18cm (7in) of sky fabric on the inside of the upper part of the bag (✂ 14). Press the top edge of the bag to form a sharp crease.

15 Turn the whole bag inside out. Using a vanishing marker or tailor's chalk, mark a line all round the inside of the bag, 7cm (2¾in) from the top edge. On the line, mark a dot 5cm (2in) to one side of the seam. Starting at this point, measure off every 10.5cm (4⅛in) along the line, marking a dot on the line each time. You should have ten dots. Adjust the positions slightly if they do not work out exactly the same distance apart. These dots are the positions for your eyelets.

16 The fabric is thick at this point so the hole-cutter supplied with eyelet kits may not work. Instead, draw round the inside of one of the eyelet backing rings, centred on each dot and, using small sharp scissors, carefully snip out the holes through all layers. It is a good idea to practise fitting the eyelets on a scrap of fabric before you embark on the actual bag.

17 Turn the bag the correct way round and fit the eyelets through the holes following the manufacturer's instructions. Thread the rope through the eyelets and knot each end.

Checkers Sleepover Quilt

The finished size of the quilt is approximately 185 x 120cm (73 x 47in) – a good size for a bed topper on a standard single bed.

Perfect for sleepovers, this quilt is not just for sleeping under, but also forms a giant draughts (checkers) board and comes complete with soft playing pieces. There is even a bag to put them in. Midnight feasts will never be the same again! We use a short cut for making the black-and-white checks for this quilt, which speeds up the piecing and makes the project easy to achieve in a weekend.

✂ you will need

Fabric quantities assume a width of at least 110cm (43in)
Seam allowance 1.5cm (⅝in)

- 180cm (71in) black fabric

- 180cm (71in) white fabric

- 170cm (67in) red fabric

- 200cm (79in) coordinating fabric for the backing

- black, red and white sewing threads

- 200 x 120cm (79 x 47in) 55g (2oz) polyester wadding (batting)

- invisible quilting thread

- 250g (10oz) soft polyester toy stuffing

- 100cm (39in) no. 4 white cotton piping cord, or similar thin rope

- see also basic equipment (page 108)

- thin card or acetate and paper for the templates, cut as follows:
14cm (5½in) square (cut from card or acetate)
68 x 17cm (26½in x 6¾in) rectangle (cut from paper)

to make the quilt

1 Cut the black, white and red fabrics according to the cutting guides (✂ 1a, 1b and 1c).

2 Take four each of the black and white checker strips and pin them, long edges together, with a seam allowance of 1.5cm (⅝in). Alternate the colours to form a rectangle of black-and-white stripes. Repeat with the remaining four checker strips to form another rectangle. Sew along the seam lines using white sewing thread and press all seams open (✂ 2).

3 Using the paper rectangle template as a guide, divide each rectangle into four 17cm (6¾in) deep strips, cutting at right angles to the seam lines (✂ 2). Reverse every other strip then pin and sew to form two checker rectangles. Press the seams open. Arrange the two rectangles so that contrasting squares abut and sew together to form a checker square using white sewing thread (✂ 3).

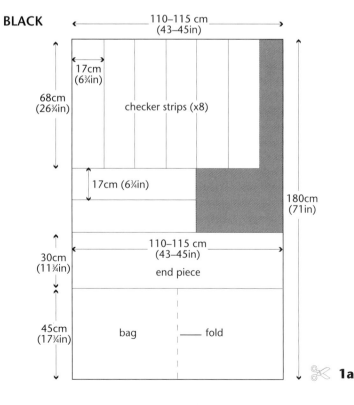

BLACK

110–115 cm (43–45in)

17cm (6¾in)

68cm (26¾in)

checker strips (x8)

17cm (6¾in)

180cm (71in)

110–115 cm (43–45in)

30cm (11¾in)

end piece

45cm (17¾in)

bag   fold

✂ **1a**

WHITE

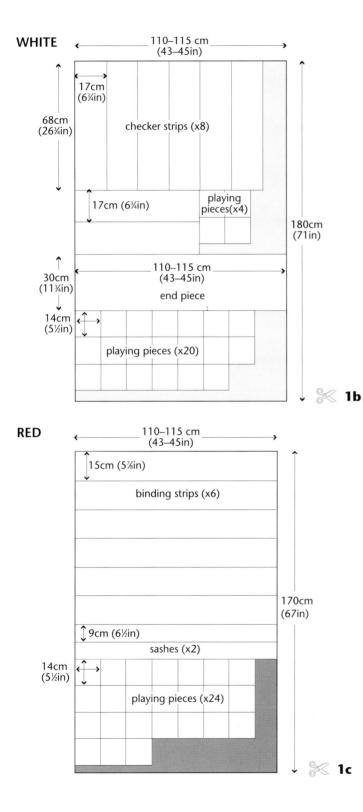

110–115 cm
(43–45in)

17cm
(6¾in)

68cm
(26¾in)

checker strips (x8)

17cm (6¾in)

playing
pieces(x4)

180cm
(71in)

110–115 cm
(43–45in)

30cm
(11¾in)

end piece

14cm
(5½in)

playing pieces (x20)

✂ **1b**

RED

110–115 cm
(43–45in)

15cm (5⅞in)

binding strips (x6)

170cm
(67in)

9cm (6½in)

sashes (x2)

14cm
(5½in)

playing pieces (x24)

✂ **1c**

cutting
lines

✂ **2**

✂ **3**

14cm
(5½in)

quilting lines

4

6 Lay the backing fabric on the floor, wrong side up (if applicable), and lay the wadding on top. Centre the quilt top on last, right side up, with an even margin of wadding extending all round. Pin-baste through all layers, avoiding any seam lines, following the instructions on page 112.

7 Using tailor's chalk on the black fabric and vanishing marker on the white fabric, mark quilting lines on the end pieces 14cm (5½in) apart (✂ 4). These are a continuation of the vertical checker lines. Machine-quilt along the lines using black thread on the black fabric and white on the white fabric, stopping at the red sashes and reversing the stitch for a few stitches to fasten off.

8 Using invisible quilting thread in the top of your machine and white in the bobbin, 'stitch-in-the-ditch' along all other seam lines (see page 112).

9 Take four of the red binding strips and join them to form two long strips. You now have two short strips and two long ones. Prepare each strip following the instructions on page 121.

10 Using red sewing thread, bind the edges of the quilt starting with the short sides, following the instructions on page 122.

4 Take the two narrower red sash strips and pin to the top and bottom of the checker square, right sides facing, raw edges level. Ensure that the squares at the bottom right- and top left-hand corners are white. Machine-stitch using red sewing thread and taking a 1.5cm (⅝in) seam. Press the seam open (✂ 4). Take the black and white end pieces. Pin and sew these onto the red sash strips and press the seams open.

5 Spread the backing fabric on the floor and smooth it out carefully. Using the quilt top as a template, cut the backing fabric 4cm (1½in) bigger all round. Cut the wadding to the same size as the backing fabric.

11 For the playing pieces, pin the 14cm (5½in) squares of fabric in pairs, right sides together. Sew all round with a 1.5cm (⅝in) seam allowance, leaving a 7.5cm (3in) gap in one side for turning and stuffing (✂ 11).

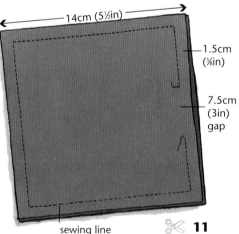

14cm (5½in)

1.5cm (⅝in)

7.5cm (3in) gap

sewing line   **11**

12 Trim the corners of each square (✄ 12) and turn right sides out, poking out the corners very gently with a closed pair of sewing scissors. Press the squares and fill each one with polyester toy stuffing until it is puffy but not hard. Oversew the opening with the appropriate coloured sewing thread using small, neat stitches (see page 117).

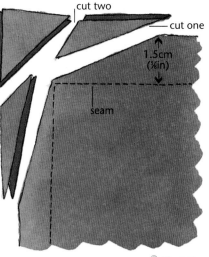

cut two

cut one

1.5cm (⅝in)

seam

✄ **12**

13 Take the rectangle of fabric for the bag and fold it in half along the short fold, right sides facing (if applicable). Press along this line. Sew the side seams. If the fabric seems prone to fray, neaten the raw edges of the side seams by pressing under a small turning on each edge and machining into place. Press the seams open. With the bag still inside out, turn the top edge of the bag under 1cm (⅜in) to the wrong side and machine-sew in place. Fold the top of the bag down a further 6cm (2⅜in) to the wrong side. Machine two lines of stitching all the way around the top of the bag, 2cm (¾in) and 4cm (1½in) from the top fold (✄ 13).

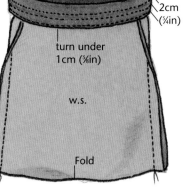

✄ **13**

2cm (¾in)

turn under 1cm (⅜in)

w.s.

Fold

14 Turn the bag right sides out. Unpick the stitching in both side seams between the stitching lines on the outside of the bag. Thread the cord through attached to a safety pin. Knot each end of the cord and use the bag for storing the playing pieces (✄ 14).

✄ **14**

Rainbow Quilt

The vibrant colours and prints used for this quilt make the project look far more complex than it is – in fact it is as basic as patchwork can be! We have used four bright prints plus single-coloured marbled fabrics in deep-blue, yellow, lime green, apple green, red, deep-red, bright pink, orange and sky blue, but you can use fewer colours if you wish. Placing the bright fabrics and prints next to contrasting colours intensifies their effect.

The finished size of the quilt is approximately 125 x 100cm (49 x 39in), which will fit a standard cot. Alternatively, you can use the quilt as a wall hanging or scale it up to fit a large cot or single bed.

✂ you will need

Fabric quantities assume a width of at least
   110cm (43in) wide
Seam allowance 1.5cm (⅝in)

- 130cm (51in) red fabric for the backing

- 80cm (32in) fabric printed with diagonal
  rainbow stripes for the binding and squares

- at least nine fat quarters of various clear
  bright marbles and prints. We used the
  following quantities for this quilt:
  40cm (16in) circles-print fabric
  40cm (16in) spectrum-print fabric
  40cm (16in) lime-green marbled fabric
  20cm (8in) orange-and-yellow striped fabric
  20cm (8in) yellow marbled fabric
  20cm (8in) bright-pink marbled fabric
  20cm (8in) deep-blue marbled fabric

20cm (8in) apple-green marbled fabric
20cm (8in) sky-blue marbled fabric
20cm (8in) orange marbled fabric
20cm (8in) red marbled fabric
20cm (8in) deep-red marbled fabric

- neutral-coloured and red sewing threads

- 125 x 100cm (49 x 39in) 55g (2oz)
  polyester wadding (batting)

- invisible quilting thread

- see also basic equipment (page 108)

- acetate for the templates, cut as follows:
  15cm (6in) square
  12cm (4¾in) square

to make the quilt

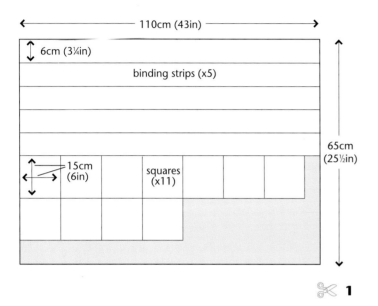

110cm (43in)

6cm (3¼in)

binding strips (x5)

65cm (25½in)

15cm (6in)

squares (x11)

✂ 1

1 Follow the cutting guide (✂ 1) to cut five 6cm (3¼in) deep strips from the width of the binding fabric, and eleven 15cm (6in) squares.

2 Using the 15cm (6in) square template, cut the following number of squares from each fabric (listed in brackets). If you want to follow a design of your own, cut eighty squares from your chosen fabrics – you should be able to cut nine squares from a fat quarter:

- circles-print fabric (eight)
- spectrum-print fabric (eight)
- lime-green marbled fabric (eight)
- orange-and-yellow striped fabric (seven)
- yellow marbled fabric (seven)
- bright-pink marbled fabric (seven)
- deep-blue marbled fabric (six)
- apple-green marbled fabric (four)
- sky-blue marbled fabric (four)

- orange marbled fabric (four)
- red marbled fabric (three)
- deep-red marbled fabric (three)

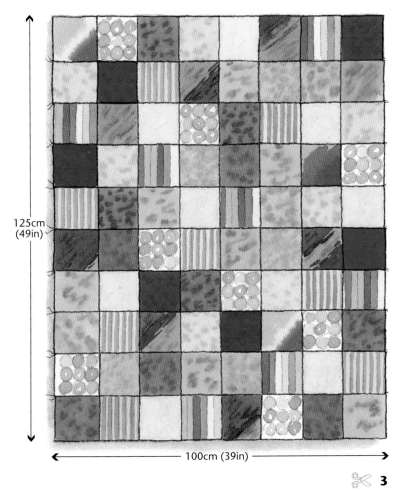

125cm (49in)

100cm (39in)

✂ **3**

4 Following the instructions on page 110, join the squares in each row taking 1.5cm (⅝in) seams and using a neutral-coloured sewing thread. For accuracy, draw seam lines on the back using the 12cm (4¾in) square and a vanishing marker. Machine-sew, then press the seams open. Mark the row number on each left-hand square.

5 Join the rows together, ensuring they are in the correct order and that the seams of each row align (see page 111). Press the seams open.

6 Use the quilt top to cut the red backing fabric 1cm (⅜in) bigger all round than the quilt top. Cut the wadding to the same size as the backing fabric.

7 Lay the backing fabric on the floor wrong side up (if applicable), lay the wadding on top, and centre the quilt top on that. There should be an even border of wadding all round. Pin-baste the three layers together, avoiding the seam lines, following the instructions on page 112.

8 Using invisible thread in the top of your machine and red thread in the bobbin quilt along all seam lines by stitching-in-the-ditch (see page 112).

9 Take the 8cm (3¼in) deep binding strips. Cut one into two equal lengths and sew each half to one of the other strips, end-to-end, so that you have two short strips and two long ones. Prepare each strip following the instructions on page 121.

10 Use a neutral-coloured sewing thread to bind the edges of the quilt, beginning with the long sides, following the instructions on page 122.

3 Following the arrangement we have used (✂ 3) lay the squares out in ten rows of eight. If you are working to your own design, make sure you spread patterns and plains evenly across the quilt; avoid having squares of the same colour close to each other and try to put contrasting fabrics next to each other where possible.

Lively Weekend

These projects are a little more time-consuming than those in the first section, with some requiring a wider range of skills.

Even though these projects are a little more demanding, they are still suitable for beginners. Each one can be completed in a weekend, provided you have obtained all the necessary materials and equipment in advance.

Pink & Lavender Cot Quilt

The finished size of the quilt is approximately 94cm (37in) square, which is fine for a crib or bassinette. On a standard cot, it also allows sufficient tuck-in for the 'feet-to-foot' position. For a quilt that fits the full length of a cot, you need to add another two or three rows of squares, for which you will need additional fabric and wadding. You can also scale the quilt up to fit a large cot or single bed.

This baby's cot quilt features terrific 50s-style novelty fabrics, set off with soft-coloured plains arranged in a 'four-square' pieced design. The bias-cut (across the weave) striped border combines the colours of the two plains and creates a strong yet subtle frame. If you wish to make a quilt in bolder colours, perhaps for a boy, there is a suggestion for an alternative colourway in maroon and turquoise.

✂ you will need

Fabric quantities assume a width of at least 115cm (45in)
Seam allowance 1cm (⅜in)

- 140cm (55in) dusty pink fabric

- 40cm (16in) lavender fabric

- 30cm (12in) each of two novelty fabrics (A) and (B)

- 20cm (8in) of a third novelty fabric (C)

- 70cm (28in) dusty pink-and-lavender striped fabric for the binding

- light-pink sewing thread

- 100cm (39in) square 55g (2oz) polyester wadding (batting)

- invisible quilting thread

- see also basic equipment (page 108)

- acetate for the templates, cut as follows:
  13cm (5⅛in) by 7.5cm (3in) rectangle
  13cm (5⅛in) square
  11cm (4⅜in) square

to make the quilt

1 Cut a 100cm (39in) square of fabric from the pink fabric for the back of the quilt and put to one side.

2 To make the checked squares, cut five 100 x 7.5cm (39 x 3in) strips from across the width of both the pink and the lavender fabrics. Sew the strips together lengthways in pairs, with a lavender strip to the left and a pink strip to the right, taking a 1cm (⅜in) seam (✂ 2). You should now have five pairs of strips. Press the seams open.

3 Using the rectangular template and tailor's chalk, carefully mark off every 7.5cm (3in) down each strip. You should have marked off 13 rectangles on each strip with a small piece left over at the end. Cut along the lines and discard the small pieces.

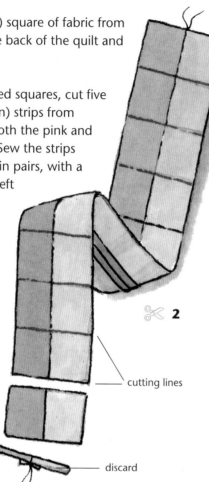

cutting lines

✂ **2**

discard

4 You will have 65 rectangles. You only need 64, so discard one. Place one rectangle in front of you, right side up, with the lavender square to the left. Place another rectangle on top of it, right side down, with the lavender square to the right. (Note that if your fabric has an obvious grain, you will need to make sure this runs from top to bottom when you assemble your squares.)

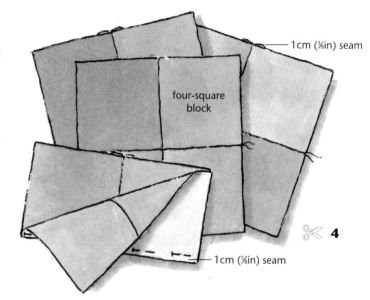

1cm (⅜in) seam

four-square block

✂ **4**

1cm (⅜in) seam

Pin the rectangles together along the bottom edge, with the pinheads to the left (✂ 4). Machine-sew together, taking a 1cm (⅜in) seam. Press the seam open. Continue in this way until you have 32 checked squares.

5 Using the 13cm (5⅛in) square template, cut twelve squares from each of fabrics (A) and (B), and eight squares from fabric (C). You may wish to 'fussy-cut' these squares ensuring each square contains an interesting part of the design. Once you have cut out the squares, centre the 11cm (4⅜in) square template on the wrong side of each of them and draw around it with tailor's chalk to give a seam allowance of 1cm (⅜in) all round.

6 Working with the fabrics right side uppermost, lay out each row of eight squares, alternating a checked square and a novelty fabric square. Each checked square should have a lavender square at the top left-hand corner.
  Row one: checked square, fabric (A), checked square, fabric (B), checked square, fabric (C), checked square, fabric (A).

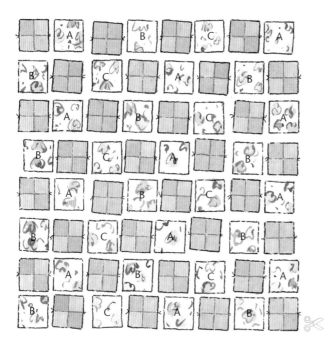

9 Using invisible thread in the top of your machine and light-pink thread in the bobbin, stitch-in-the-ditch along the five main vertical and horizontal seams (see page 112).

10 Using the pink-and-lavender striped fabric, make 158cm (160in) of 10cm (4in) wide bias binding following the instructions on page 121. Cut the binding into four 100cm (39½in) lengths. Prepare each strip following the instructions on page 121.

11 Using light-pink sewing thread, bind the quilt, beginning with the top and bottom edges, following the instructions on page 122.

Row two: fabric (B), checked square, fabric (C), checked square, fabric (A), checked square, fabric (B) (✂ 6). Repeat this sequence three more times. Note that if the fabric has a directional or one-way pattern, the novelty squares must all be the correct way round.

7 Following the instructions on page 110, join the squares in each row taking 1.5cm (⅝in) seams and using the marked seam line for accuracy. Machine-sew, then press the seams open. Mark the row number on each left-hand square, either in the seam allowance or by pinning a piece of paper to it.

8 Use the quilt top to cut the dusty pink backing fabric 3cm (1¼in) wider all round. Cut the wadding to the same size as the backing. Lay the backing fabric on the floor wrong side up (if applicable), lay the wadding on top, and centre the quilt top on that. There should be an even border of wadding all round. Pin-baste the three layers together, avoiding the seam lines, following the instructions on page 112.

Alternative
The pink and lavender quilt is especially suitable for little girls. For a bolder colour scheme, use dark turquoise and maroon fabric for the checked squares, a co-ordinating turquoise stripe for the border and figurative prints in toning colours.

Springtime Baby Bag

The finished size of the bag (excluding the handles) is approximately 54 x 43cm (21¼ x 17¾in).

This roomy baby bag is sure to delight new mums and dads. Charming fussy-cut motifs coordinate with sunny gingham squares, creating an eye-catching patchwork design. Practical interior pockets are great for carrying baby essentials and, provided you pre-wash the fabrics, you should be able to launder the bag without it shrinking. For practicality and strength, we used a slightly heavier weight fabric than you would normally use for a bed quilt.

✂ you will need

Fabric quantities assume a width of at least 154cm (60in) unless stated otherwise*
Seam allowance 1.5cm (⅝in)

- 71cm (28in) fabric with pictorial motifs (the exact size will depend on the nature of the motifs and the distance between them)

- 130cm (51in) yellow gingham fabric

- 160cm (63in) firm iron-on interfacing, 91cm (36in) wide*

- cream and primrose-yellow sewing threads

- 91cm (36in) by 60cm (24in) iron-on wadding (batting)

- large wooden or plastic button in a toning colour, about 4cm (1½in) diameter

- see also basic equipment (page 108)

- thin card or acetate for the templates, cut as follows:
  21cm (8¼in) square from acetate
  18cm (7in) square
  15 x 4cm (6 x 1½in) rectangle
  8.8cm (3¼in) right-angled triangle
  (see page 132)

to make the bag

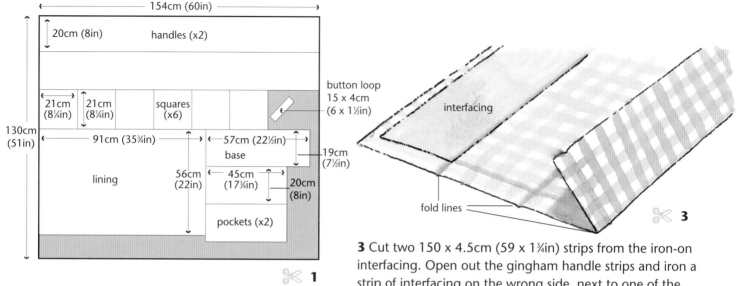

1 Fussy-cut six scenes or motifs from the printed fabric using the 21cm (8¼in) square acetate template. Cut out all the pieces from the yellow gingham following the cutting guide (✂ 1). Use the rectangle template to cut the button loop on the bias (diagonally, across the grain of the fabric).

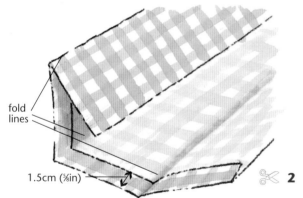

2 Press each handle strip in half lengthways, wrong sides facing (if applicable). Open out the strip again. Press the ends up 1.5cm (⅝in) then press the long raw edges to the centre fold (✂ 2).

3 Cut two 150 x 4.5cm (59 x 1¾in) strips from the iron-on interfacing. Open out the gingham handle strips and iron a strip of interfacing on the wrong side, next to one of the outside edges, following the interfacing manufacturer's instructions (✂ 3).

4 Take each strip and refold it as for step 2. Press, and pin down the centre line of each strip. Machine-sew, using top stitch, 1cm (⅜in) in from each folded edge and across the end of each strip, using primrose-yellow thread.

5 Following the instructions on page 11, join together four rows of gingham and printed fabric squares using cream sewing thread. (For accuracy use the 18cm (7⅛in) square template to mark the seam allowance:
    Row one: print, gingham, print
    Row two: gingham, print, gingham
    Row three: print, gingham, print
    Row four: gingham, print, gingham

6 Now join rows one and two to form the front of the bag and rows three and four to form the back. Use the triangle template as a guide to trim a triangle from each bottom corner of the two panels.

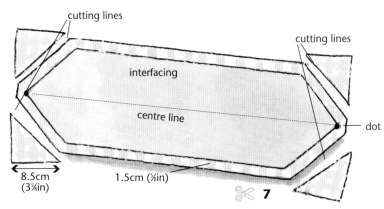

cutting lines

cutting lines

interfacing

centre line

dot

8.5cm
(3⅜in)

1.5cm (⅝in)

✂ **7**

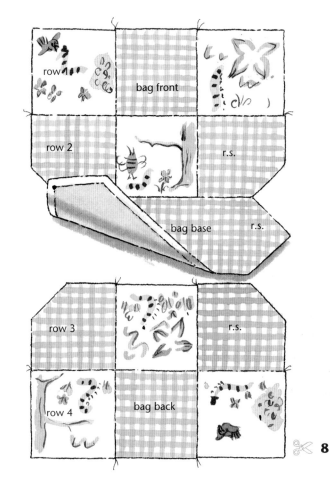

row 1

bag front

row 2

r.s.

bag base

r.s.

row 3

r.s.

row 4

bag back

✂ **8**

7 Take the base of the bag and an erasable marker and, on the wrong side of the fabric, mark a dot at each end on the centre line, 1.5cm (⅝in) in from the short edges. Use the triangle template (page 132) to mark and cut a triangle from each corner. Cut two pieces of interfacing 53 x 16cm (20¾ x 6¼in) and, again, trim a triangle from each corner using the template. Take one piece of interfacing (reserve the other for later) and centre it on the wrong side of the base of the bag. Iron in place following the manufacturer's instructions (✂ 7).

8 To assemble the bag, arrange the bag front, the base and the back as shown in ✂ 8. Ensure that rows three and four are upside down in relation to rows one and two. With right sides together, pin, then sew, the base – still using cream sewing thread – to the front and back along the bottom straight seam lines. Do not press the seams open.

9 Place the front of the bag against the back, right sides together. Fold the base in half and position between the front and back panels. Fold one half of the base up towards you and pin, then sew, a 1.5cm (⅝in) seam along the diagonal edges, from the marked dot to the lower edge of the base (✂ 9). Turn the bag over and repeat on the other side.

10 Sew the sides of the bag from the marked dot up to the top edges on either side. Press the seam open and turn the bag right sides out.

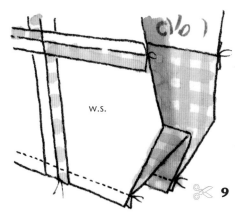

w.s.

✂ **9**

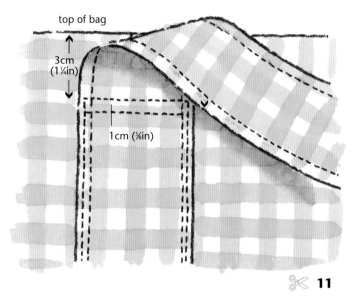

top of bag

3cm (1¼in)

1cm (⅜in)

✂ **11**

11 Position the handle strips a third of the way across the bag on either side so they are centred over the vertical patchwork seams. The ends should butt up to each other on the base of the bag. Ensuring the straps are not twisted, pin them in place and, using primrose-yellow sewing thread, stitch between the top stitching and the edge of the strap, stopping 3cm (1⅜in) short of the top of the bag and sewing horizontally across the strap at this point. To strengthen, sew across the strap again 1.5cm (⅝in) lower (✂ 11).

12 Fold the lining fabric in half with short edges together. Measure 8cm (3⅛in) either side of the centre line and draw parallel lines to mark out the base of the lining. Centre the reserved interfacing on the wrong side of the base and iron in place (see ✂ 12). Cut the iron-on wadding to 88 x 53cm (34½ x 20¾in) and centre it on the wrong side of the lining, over the interfacing. Iron in place following the manufacturer's instructions.

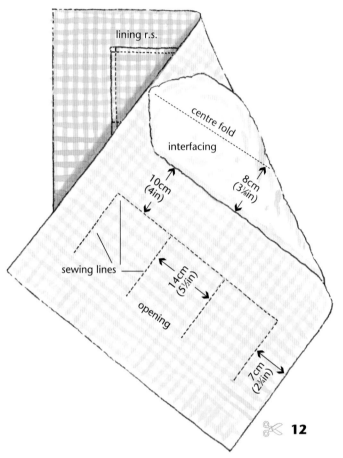

lining r.s.

centre fold

interfacing

10cm (4in)

8cm (3⅛in)

sewing lines

14cm (5½in)

opening

7cm (2¾in)

✂ **12**

13 Turn one long edge of each pocket piece down 1cm (⅜in) then another 1cm (⅜in). Pin then sew. Press 1.5cm (⅝in) turnings around the other three edges. Position the pocket pieces on either side of the base of the lining, with the bottom of each piece towards the centre (✂ 12). Sew in place using primrose-yellow sewing thread. Stitch each pocket piece at 14cm (5½in) intervals to form three pockets. Reinforce the points of strain at the top of each pocket by sewing several short stitches over one another and at right angles to the seam line.

14 Follow the instructions in step 7 to mark dots on the wrong side. With the pockets on the inside, sew along the four diagonal seams as in step 9, stopping at the dots. Trim the corners to match the outer bag. Sew the side seams as in step 10 but leave a 20cm (8in) gap in the centre of one seam.

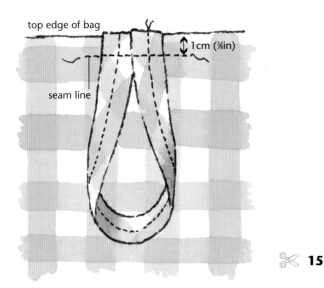

top edge of bag

1cm (⅜in)

seam line

✂ **15**

15 Make the button loop by folding the fabric in half lengthways and pressing the sides to the centre again. Still using primrose-yellow sewing thread, machine-sew down the centre of the folded strip. Form a loop and position it at the top edge of the front of the bag with the loop pointing downwards and the raw ends level with the top of the bag. Machine-sew in place 1cm (⅜in) from the top of the bag (✂ 15).

16 Pin the handles to the side of the bag, out of the way of the seam allowance along the top edge. Turn the bag inside out, so that the lining is showing, but the pockets are on the inside. Make sure the top raw edges of the bag are level with the top edges of the lining and that the side seams align. Pin and sew all round the top edge, sewing over the loop ends as you do so.

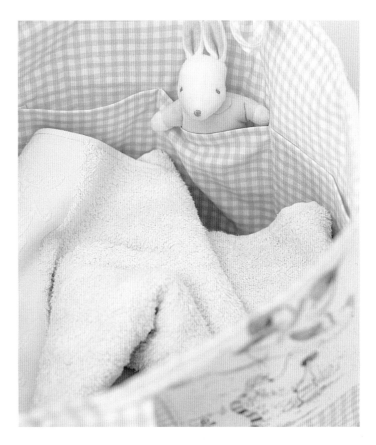

17 Pull the bag right sides out through the gap in the lining. Sew up the opening and press the top edge. Top stitch 1cm (⅜in) from the top edge.

18 Using primrose-yellow sewing thread, sew the button on the centre line at the front of the bag with the centre of the button 4cm (1½in) from the top edge.

Alternatives
Choose different fabrics; you may prefer a combination of a check and a plain, perhaps in a more 'adult' colourway.

Patchwork Cat

This cuddly ginger tom is sure to be a firm favourite with children. Simple to make from fabric offcuts and remnants, this cat has a patchwork front, a plain back, an embroidered face and a smart bow. If you are short of time or do not feel confident enough to tackle the embroidery, you can easily draw the cat's features with a fabric pen instead.

The finished size of the cat is approximately 50 x 38 cm (20 x 15in).

✂ you will need

Seam allowance 1cm (⅜in)

- 50 x 110cm (20 x 43in) bright-yellow fabric with textured print

- 20 x 110cm (8 x 43in) ochre fabric with tiny ginger circles

- 15 x 50cm (6 x 20in) mottled ginger fabric

- 15 x 50cm (6 x 20in) mottled tan fabric

- 15 x 40cm (6 x 16in) ochre fabric

- 15 x 50cm (6 x 20in) shot khaki fabric

- 15 x 40cm (6 x 16in) shot brown fabric

- 15 x 20cm (6 x 8in) blue-and-white spotted fabric for bow

- scraps of red-and-white tiny check fabric

- 20 x 91cm (8 x 36in) firm iron-on interfacing

- 15 x 46cm (6 x 18in) fusible webbing

- bright-red machine-embroidery thread

- one skein each of dark-brown and mid-blue stranded embroidery thread

- mid-blue and brown or black fine permanent marker pen

- two black oval buttons about 1.7cm (⅝in) long plus two small shirt buttons with two holes in, or a scrap of firmly woven black felt

- black sewing thread

- 600g (20oz) polyester fibre toy stuffing

- see also basic equipment (page 108)

- thin card or acetate for the templates, cut as follows:
  11cm (4⅜in) square
  9cm (3½in) square

- two sheets of thin 29.7 x 42.2cm (11½ x 16½in) size paper (A2) for making the patterns on page 133

Note Buttons should be used for the eyes of this cat only if it is to be given to children over three years old. For children under this age, or where younger children live in the same house, use felt for the eyes.

to make the patchwork cat

1 Using the A2 paper, square up the patterns for the cat's body, the base of the cushion and the cat's tail, or enlarge to A2 size on a photocopier (see page 119).

2 Reverse the cat's body pattern and, following the line of grain on the pattern, cut one cat's back from the bright-yellow fabric. From the same fabric, cut the base and, using the template, five 11cm (4⅜in) squares. Using the ginger circles fabric economically, cut four 11cm (4⅜in) squares and two tail pieces – one a mirror image of the other.

3 Trim off 1cm (⅜in) all round the base pattern and cut a piece of iron-on interfacing to this shape. Centre the interfacing on the wrong side of the base fabric and iron in place following the manufacturer's instructions.

4 Using the large template, cut four 11cm (4⅜in) squares from the mottled ginger and tan, and shot khaki fabrics and three from the ochre and shot brown fabrics.

5 Following the instructions on page 110, join the squares together in rows in the following order, with a 1cm (⅜in) seam, and pressing all the seams open. For accuracy, draw seam lines on the back of each using the 9cm (3½in) square and a vanishing marker. Machine-sew, then press, the seams open. Mark the row number on each left-hand square:

> **Row one:** ochre, tan, ginger
> **Row two:** ginger circles, khaki, bright yellow, ochre
> **Row three:** ginger, tan, ginger circles, brown
> **Row four:** tan, khaki, bright yellow, ginger, khaki
> **Row five:** bright yellow, ginger circles, ginger, khaki, bright yellow
> **Row six:** brown, ochre, bright yellow, ginger circles, ginger
> **Row seven:** brown, khaki, tan

6 Join all the rows together in the correct order. The first six rows should align on the right-hand side. The last row is centred below the sixth row, with one fewer square at either end (✂ 6).

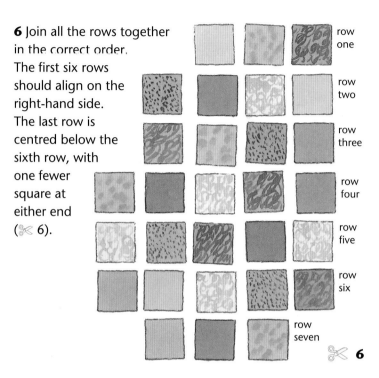

row one
row two
row three
row four
row five
row six
row seven

✂ **6**

7 Turn the patchwork through 45 degrees so the squares become diamonds and there is a mottled ginger diamond at the very top. Place the cat pattern on the patchwork, right side up (✂ 7), ensuring that all parts of the pattern are on the fabric. Pin the pattern to the fabric and cut out the cat shape.

✂ **7**

8 Transfer the markings for the cat's face to the fabric (see page 119). Iron fusible webbing to the back of the red-and-white check fabric. Trace off and cut out the shapes for the ears, nose and tongue. Iron onto the face. Using red embroidery thread, machine-embroider around the edges of the shapes using satin stitch, and sew the mouth.

9 Machine-embroider the whiskers with dark-brown embroidery thread, using backstitch. With the black or dark brown fabric pen, mark dots on either side of the mouth as shown on the pattern (see page 133). Heat-set the dots, following the pen manufacturer's instructions.

10 Iron fusible webbing onto the back of the blue-and-white spotted fabric and cut the bow from it. Iron in place on the cat's neck following the manufacturer's instructions, then mark the embroidery lines on the bow. Machine-embroider the main details in satin stitch, using blue embroidery thread. Carefully draw in the finer details using the blue fabric marker pen, as shown on the pattern (see page 133). Heat-set the pen markings, following the manufacturer's instructions.

11 For children over three years old, sew on the button eyes using strong black thread. Sewing through the small buttons on the back of the fabric to ensure the eyes are held firmly in place. For younger children, cut oval eyes from black felt.

12 Pin the two parts of the tail together, right sides facing, and sew round all sides apart from the straight end. Turn right sides out, press and stuff. Tack the tail in place onto the side seam on the front section of the cat (✂ 12).

13 Pin, then sew, the front and back sections of the cat together, with right sides facing, but excluding the base. You will catch the tail in place as you sew. Turn the cat right sides out and press flat.

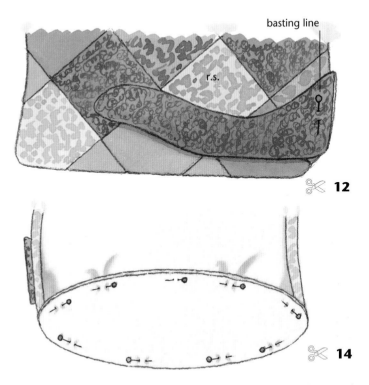

basting line
r.s.
✂ **12**

✂ **14**

14 Turn the cat inside out again. Fold the base into four and mark the quarters in the seam allowance. Fold the cat in half from side to side, so the seams meet, and mark the halfway point in the seam allowance along the base line. Pin, then stitch, the base in place, matching up the dots, and leaving a 15cm (6in) hole for turning (✂ 14). Turn right sides out and press. Fill the cat with polyester fibre stuffing then oversew the opening closed (see page 117).

Alternatives
Instead of ginger fabrics, you could use blue-and-white prints and plains. You can omit the sewn bow and tie a real bow around the neck. To make the cat into a doorstop, fill a freezer bag with sand, knot, then put it into another freezer bag and knot. Insert the bag into the base of the cat once you have nearly stuffed it.

Safari Wall Pockets

The finished size of the wall hanging is approximately 127 x 84cm (50 x 33in), excluding the loops. You can make it smaller if you wish with just two rows of pockets, in which case the panel will be about 70cm (28in) deep, again, excluding the loops.

This wall hanging is the perfect home for all those small soft toys that otherwise end up strewn around the bedroom or lost at the bottom of the toy box. We have used a cheerful animal print, but you could choose any fabric with large motifs. Furnishing-weight fabric is recommended for this project as the pockets need to be sturdy enough to take everyday use.

✂ you will need

Fabric quantities assume a width of at least 110cm (43in)
Seam allowance 1.5cm (⅝in)

- 280cm (110in) yellow-green striped fabric

- 150cm (59in) jungle fabric with widely spaced motifs

- 140cm (55in) light-green striped fabric

- 60cm (24in) small giraffe-print fabric

- 130 x 90cm (51 x 36in) 55g (2oz) wadding (batting)

- 1.8cm (1¹⁄₁₆in) tape-maker (optional)

- invisible quilting thread

- light-green and ochre sewing threads

- 91cm (36in) long wooden curtain pole

- see also basic equipment (page 108)

- thin paper or tracing paper for the patterns, cut as follows:
  23 x 7.5cm (9 x 3in): fabric (A)
  23 x 11cm (9 x 4⅜in): fabric (B)
  23cm (9in) square: fabric (C)
  23 x 18cm (9 x 7in): fabric (D)

Note The design of these pockets is fairly robust. However, they are not suitable for very heavy items. Choose a curtain pole that attaches firmly to its wall brackets, and ensure the pole is attached firmly to the wall with suitable fixings.

to make the wall hanging

1 Cut the yellow-green striped fabric widthways into two equal 140cm (55in) lengths. Reserve one of the pieces for the backing. Follow the cutting guide (✄ 1) to cut eight strips from the remaining yellow-green striped fabric. Use the same cutting guide to cut three large strips and three small strips from the light-green striped fabric.

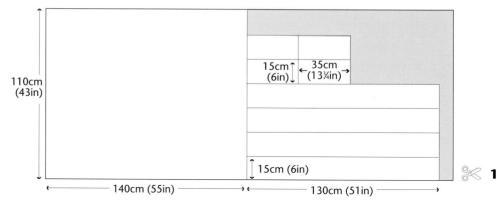

110cm (43in)

15cm (6in)

35cm (13¾in)

15cm (6in)

140cm (55in)

130cm (51in)

✄ 1

2 Take the seven large strips and, starting and ending with a yellow-green one, pin the strips together, right sides facing and long edges together, alternating the fabric colours. Using light-green sewing thread, machine-sew the strips together, taking a 1.5cm (⅝in) seam. Press the seams open (✄ 2).

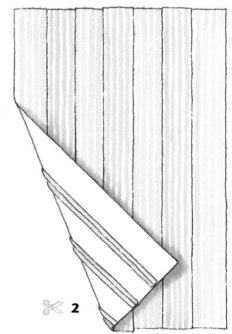

✄ 2

3 Using the sewn strips as a template, cut the backing fabric and wadding to the same size. Lay out the backing fabric, wrong side up (if applicable), smoothing out any creases. Place the wadding on top and the sewn strips on top of that. Pin-baste the three layers together, avoiding the seams, and following the instructions on page 112.

4 Stitch-in-the-ditch along the seam lines using invisible quilting thread in the top of the machine and light-green in the bobbin (see page 112).

5 Cut five 7cm (2¾in) deep strips from the whole width of the giraffe print fabric. Cut one strip into two and join each half, end-to-end, to one of the other strips. Press the seams open. Prepare each strip following the instructions on page 121.

6 Using ochre sewing thread, bind the edges of the quilt beginning with the short ends, and following the instructions on page 122.

7 Using invisible thread in the top of your machine and light-green thread in the bobbin, stitch-in-the-ditch along the pinned binding seams following the instructions on page 112.

8 To make the pockets, fussy-cut four pandas and four giraffes (or similar) using template (C), and four lions and four elephants (or similar) using template (D). From the leafy parts of the leftover fabric (between the animals), cut eight pieces using template (A) and twelve pieces using template (b). Pin the pieces, right sides together to form four rows as follows (✂ 8):

> **Row one:** piece (A), lion, piece (B), giraffe, piece (B), elephant, piece (B), panda, piece (A)
> **Row two:** piece (A), panda, piece (B), lion, piece (B), giraffe, piece (B), elephant, piece (A)
> **Row three:** piece (A), elephant, piece (B), panda, piece (B), lion, piece (B), giraffe, piece (A)
> **Row four:** piece (A), giraffe, piece (B), elephant, piece (B), panda, piece (B), lion, piece (A)

Ensure the animal motifs are all the correct way up, then machine-sew using light-green sewing thread and press all seams open.

✂ **8**

9 Press the long top edge of each strip 1cm (⅜in) towards the wrong side, then press under again. Machine-sew in place using light-green sewing thread. Cut four 3.6cm (1⅜in) deep strips from across the width of the giraffe-print fabric. Pass through a tape-maker (see page 109), ironing the strips at the same time. (Trimming the end of each strip to a slight point will help the fabric through the tape maker.) If you have not got a bias-tape maker, press the strips in half lengthways, open out and press the raw edges to the centre. Do not open up the tape, but fold it in half lengthways along the top edge of the pockets (✂ 9). Pin and machine-sew through all layers using ochre sewing thread.

✂ **9**

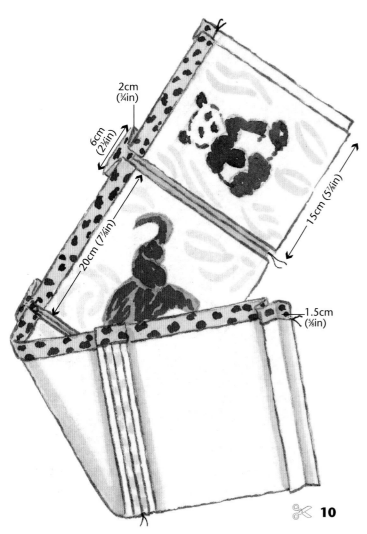

2cm (¾in)

6cm (2⅜in)

20cm (7⅞in)

15cm (5⅞in)

1.5cm (⅝in)

✂ **10**

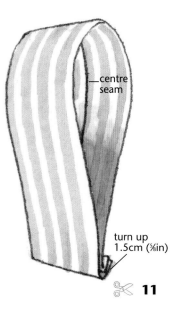

centre seam

turn up 1.5cm (⅝in)

✂ **11**

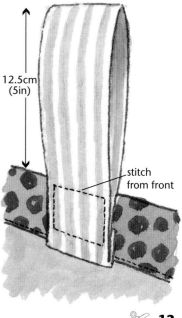

12.5cm (5in)

stitch from front

✂ **12**

11 To make the loops for hanging, take the seven small strips of striped fabric and fold in half lengthways, wrong sides together and raw edges level. Pin along the raw edge and sew to form tubes. Press the seams open, then turn right sides out and press with the seam in the centre. Fold in half widthways with the seam on the inside and the raw ends level. Turn the raw ends under 1.5cm (⅝in), press, then stitch (✂ 11).

12 Working on the back of the quilt, position each loop along the top edge, centred above its corresponding colour section. The turning on the loop should face the back of the quilt and should lie across the binding seam line. (Ensure the loops are level at the top, otherwise they will not take the weight evenly on the hanging pole.) Machine-sew each strip in place by stitching a rectangle on the right side of the binding – that is from the front of the quilt (✂ 12).

10 Taking each row of pockets in turn, use the seam where one panel of fabric joins the next to press a series of box pleats along the length of the row (✂ 10). Form the end pleats by bringing the edge of the 6cm (2⅜in) section across to within 2cm (¾in) of the raw edge, and pressing. Then press the raw edges 1.5cm (⅝in) to the wrong side, so that a 5mm (³⁄₁₆in) strip projects beyond the pleat (✂ 10). Pin, then tack, all pleats in place, press under and tack 1.5cm (⅝in) along the bottom edge of each strip.

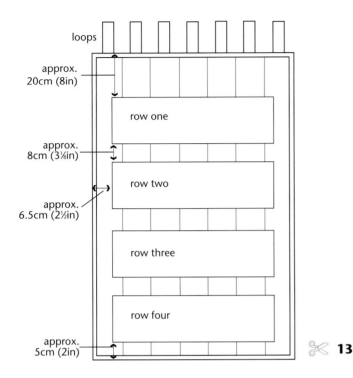

loops

approx. 20cm (8in)

row one

approx. 8cm (3⅛in)

row two

approx. 6.5cm (2½in)

row three

row four

approx. 5cm (2in)

✂ **13**

13 Position each row of pockets on the quilt and stitch in place (✂ 13). When sewing between the box pleats, ensure you do not catch the edges. When sewing close to the binding, lift the presser foot with the needle still in the fabric, and remove the pleat from under the presser foot, snipping any tacking if necessary, then tuck the pleat back underneath and continue sewing. Sew backwards and forwards twice at points of strain.

14 Decide on the position of the quilt on the wall (the top pockets must be easy for a child to reach without stretching). The curtain pole needs to be approximately 11cm (4⅜in) above your chosen position for the top edge of the quilt. Fix pole brackets firmly to the wall using appropriate fixings. Slot the loops onto the pole and hang the quilt.

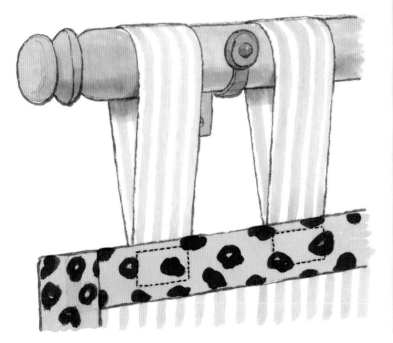

Alternative

Instead of using fabric with widely spaced motifs, you can use an all-over jungle print to make the pockets for this wall hanging. It should measure 100 x 110cm (39 x 43in) and should be cut into four 106 x 23cm (41¾ x 9in) strips from across the width.

Take the first and third rows and measure from the left as follows, making a small mark in the top and bottom seam allowances, and taking the next measurement from that: 6cm (2⅜in), 20cm (7⅞in), 8cm (3⅛in), 15cm (5⅞in), 8cm (3⅛in), 20cm (7⅞in), 8cm (3⅛in), 15cm (5⅞in), 6cm (2⅜in). Reverse the order for the second and fourth rows, so: 6cm (2⅜in), 15cm (5⅞in), 8cm (3⅛in), 20cm (7⅞in), 8cm (3⅛in), 15cm (5⅞in), 8cm (3⅛in), 20cm (7⅞in), 6cm (2⅜in).

Draw a dot in the seam allowance to mark the centre line of each 8cm (3⅛in) section. Press these into box pleats by bringing the edges of the front pocket section across to the centre line (✂ 10). Follow steps 10 to 14 to complete the project.

Baby's Love Blanket

Ideal for use in a buggy (baby carriage) or with a car seat, this little quilt makes a perfect gift for a newborn. Because the blanket is so small, it doesn't require complex quilting – the three quilted hearts are sufficient if you use good-quality bonded wadding – and the fabrics used make a refreshing change from the usual baby colours. This quilt would also make a very smart topper for a doll's bed.

The finished size of the quilt is approximately 50 x 42cm (20 x 16½in). Alternatively you can scale it up to fit a large cot or single bed (see page 131), or use it as a wall hanging (see page 124).

✂ you will need

Fabric quantities assume a width of at least 110cm (43in)
Seam allowance 1cm (⅜in)

- 50cm (20in) dark-pink fabric for the backing

- 20cm (8in) pink marbled fabric for binding

- 20cm (8in) lime-green fabric

- 20cm (8in) green-and-white small gingham check

- 20cm (8in) pink batik heart-motif fabric

- 10cm (4in) fusible webbing, 91cm (36in) wide

- dark-pink, shaded (space-dyed) machine-embroidery thread

- 56cm (22in) long by 46cm (18in) wide 55g (2oz) polyester wadding (batting)

- light-green and dark-pink sewing threads

- one skein lime-green stranded embroidery thread

- one skein dark-pink stranded embroidery thread

- see also basic equipment (page 108)

- thin card or acetate for the templates, cut as follows:
  heart (see page 132)
  12cm (4¾in) square
  10cm (4in) square
  7cm (2¾in) square
  5cm (2in) square

61

to make the blanket

1 Cut a 56 x 46cm (22 x 18in) rectangle from dark-pink fabric for the backing, and set aside. Cut four 5cm (2in) wide binding strips from the pink marbled fabric, two 43cm (17in) long and two 56cm (22in) long.

2 Using the 12cm (4¾in) and 7cm (2¾in) square templates, cut the fabric as follows:
- lime-green fabric: three large squares and eight small ones
- dark-pink fabric: two large squares and six small ones
- pink marbled fabric: two large squares and five small ones
- green-and-white gingham fabric: three large squares and eight small ones
- batik heart-motif fabric: two large squares and five small ones

3 Iron a 9cm (3½in) square of fusible webbing to the back of the remnants of the dark-pink fabric, and a 9 x 18cm (3½ x 7in) rectangle to the back of the remnants of the pink marbled fabric. Using the heart template cut one heart from the dark-pink fabric and two from the pink marbled fabric. Centre the dark-pink heart on a large lime-green square and the pink marbled hearts on two green-and-white gingham squares. Iron in place, following the manufacturer's instructions. Use satin stitch to machine-sew around the hearts using pink-shaded machine-embroidery thread or, if you prefer, hand-embroider just inside the edge of each heart at step 10.

4 Lay out the large squares in rows as follows (✂ 4):
> **Row one:** lime-green square, dark-pink square, gingham square
> **Row two:** pink marbled square, gingham square, batik square
> **Row three:** lime-green square, dark-pink square, lime-green square
> **Row four:** batik square, gingham square, pink marbled square

5 Following the instructions on page 110, pin, then machine-sew, the three large squares in each row, using light-green sewing thread and taking a 1cm (⅜in) seam. For accuracy, use the 10cm (4in) square template to mark the seam lines. Press the seams open.

6 Join the small squares to form four border strips as follows, pinning a scrap of paper with the strip number on the left-hand square of each strip, see page 110. For accuracy, use the 5cm (2in) square template to mark the seam lines:
> **Strip one:** pink marble, lime green, dark pink, gingham, batik, lime green, pink marble, gingham
> **Strip two:** gingham, pink marble, lime green, batik, gingham, dark pink, lime green, batik
> **Strip three:** gingham, batik, lime green, dark pink,

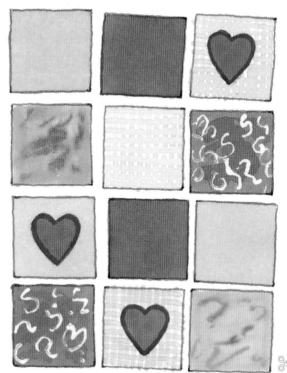

✂ 4

gingham, pink marble, lime green, dark pink
Strip four: dark pink, lime green, batik, gingham, pink marble, lime green, dark pink, gingham

Press all seams open.

7 Pin strip one to the left-hand side of the centre panel, right sides facing with the small pink marble square at the top, and aligning seams where appropriate. Pin strip two to the right-hand side of the centre panel, with the small gingham square at the top. Machine-sew the strips in place using light-green sewing thread, and taking a 1cm (⅜in) seam. Press the seams open.

✂ **8**

8 Pin strip three across the top of the panel, with the gingham square on the left. Pin strip four along the bottom of the panel, with the dark-pink square on the left (✂ 8). Machine-sew and press the seams open.

9 Using the quilt top as a template, cut the dark-pink backing fabric and the wadding to the same size. Place the backing fabric wrong side up (if applicable) with the wadding on top and the quilt top on that. Ensure each layer is smoothed out carefully and that the edges align. Pin-baste the quilt following the instructions on page 112.

✂ **10**

10 Centre the heart template on the top-left large square and draw around it using a vanishing marker. Repeat on the two large squares on the same diagonal (✂ 10). Hand-quilt the marked hearts through all layers with tiny running stitches and three strands of embroidery thread (see page 115). Use pink on the lime-green squares and lime-green on the gingham squares. If you omitted the satin stitching in step 3, sew in the same way, just inside the edges of the bonded hearts, using lime-green thread.

11 Prepare each binding strip (see page 121 for instructions).

12 Bind the quilt, starting with the short ends and oversewing the binding in place by hand on the back, using dark-pink sewing thread (see page 122 for instructions).

Country Boy's Quilt

The finished size of the quilt is approximately 197 x 148cm (77½ x 58in), which will fit a standard single bed.

Circles of patchwork act as windows onto a boy's own farm world of tractors and trailers. Sewing on the fabric circles does the job of quilting at the same time. The plain materials are slightly 'shot', giving depth and interest to the quilt, while the subtle colours tone well with the tractor motifs.

✂ you will need

Fabric quantities assume a width of at least 115cm (45in)
Seam allowance 1.5cm (⅝in)

- 170cm (67in) smoky-plum fabric

- 170cm (67in) paprika-red fabric

- 20cm (8in) moss-green fabric

- 200cm (79in) blue sheeting for the backing

- 100cm (39in) checked fabric for binding

- 20cm (8in) each of three tractor or transport fabrics, on red, green and blue backgrounds

- plum-coloured, red, green and blue sewing threads

- 200 x 150cm (79 x 59in) 55g (2oz) or 115g (4oz) polyester wadding (batting)

- invisible quilting thread

- 60cm (24in) medium-weight soft iron-on interfacing 91cm (36in) wide

- see also basic equipment (page 108)

- acetate for the templates, cut as follows:
  15.5cm (6in) diameter circle
  14.5cm (5¾in) diameter circle

to make the quilt

1 Cut a 163 x 114cm (64 x 45in) rectangle from the plum fabric. Cut two 163 x 18cm (64 x 7in) strips, and two 115 x 18cm (45¼ x 7in) strips from the length of the red fabric. Cut four 18cm (7in) squares from the moss-green fabric.

2 Join the two longer red strips to the long sides of the plum rectangle, taking a 1.5cm (⅝in) seam, and using plum-coloured sewing thread. Press the seams open.

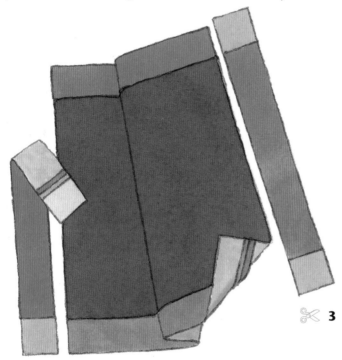

✂ **3**

3 Join a green square to each end of the shorter red strips and press the seams open (✂ 3). Sew these strips to the top and bottom of the plum rectangle, right sides facing and seam lines matching up. Press the seams open.

4 Using the quilt top as a template, cut the backing fabric 2cm (¾in) bigger all round. Cut the wadding to the same size as the backing fabric. Lay the backing fabric on the floor, wrong side up (if applicable), then lay the wadding

on that, and centre the quilt top on that, with an equal border of wadding showing all round. Pin-baste through all three layers, avoiding the seam lines, and following the instructions on page 112.

5 Stitch-in-the-ditch along all seam lines using invisible quilting thread in the top of the machine and blue in the bobbin, (see instructions on page 112). Leave pins in place.

6 Use the check fabric to make two 200 x 10cm (79 x 4in) and two 155 x 10cm (61 x 4in) bias strips, joining where necessary (see page 121). Prepare each binding strip following the instructions on page 121.

7 Use blue thread to bind the quilt, starting with the short ends, and following the instructions on page 122.

8 Use the larger template to fussy-cut eight 15.5cm (6in) diameter circles from each of the tractor or transport fabrics.

9 Cut 24 circles, 14.5cm (5¾in) diameter, from the interfacing. Centre an interfacing circle, adhesive side down, onto the back of each fabric circle and press in place following the manufacturer's instructions.

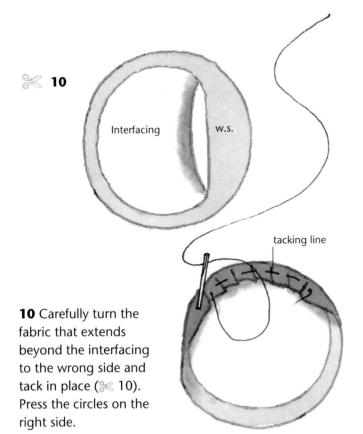

10 Carefully turn the fabric that extends beyond the interfacing to the wrong side and tack in place (✂ 10). Press the circles on the right side.

11 Position the circles on the plum fabric with four circles across the fabric and six down (✂ 11a). The circles in the horizontal rows should be spaced approximately 11cm (4¼in) from each other at their widest points, and from the edge of the plum fabric. The circles in the vertical rows should be spaced approximately 10.5cm (4⅛in) from each other and from the edge of the plum fabric. Ensure the motifs on the fabric are all the same way up. Pin the circles in place with small quilting safety pins, removing any other pins that are in the way. Use six pins per circle (✂ 11b).

12 Machine-sew around each circle using matching sewing thread. You will have to manoeuvre the quilt to do this, and you may find it easier to sew each circle in two stages, cutting the thread and rotating the quilt in between.

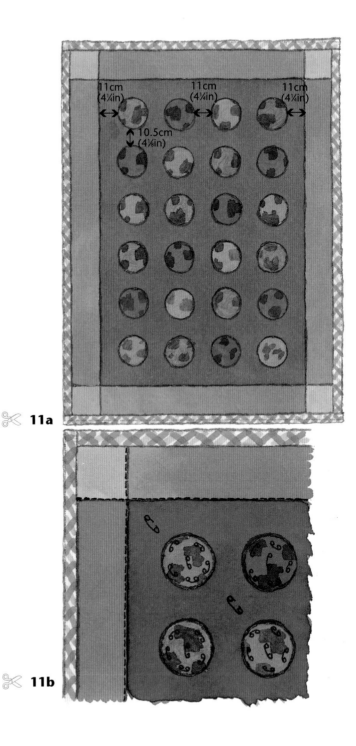

'Me and Mine' Quilt

The finished size of the quilt is approximately 192 x 145cm (75½ x 57in) and will fit a standard single bed. You can easily adjust the size by reducing or increasing the background fabric. For larger quilts, use wide-width fabric and add extra pictures. You can also use the quilt as a playmat or convert it into a wall hanging.

This quilt is a collage of a child's drawings and tells the story of its owner. Images can include pictures of the child, a favourite pet, toys and interests, the family home, close relatives and so on. Words may also be included, such as the child's name, which can make use of decorative letters. Older children might even like to take part in making the quilt by embroidering a rectangle or two of their own.

✂ you will need

Fabric quantities assume a width of at least 145cm (57in) unless stated otherwise*
Seam allowance 1.5cm (⅝in)

- 400cm (160½in) blue-and-white gingham fabric for the quilt top and backing

- 200cm (79in) blue fabric for the binding

- 100cm (39in) white fabric (this needs to be of sufficient thickness for the gingham pattern to not show through when placed underneath)

- 200 x 145cm (79 x 57in) 55g (2oz) polyester wadding (batting)

- selection of the child's drawings, relating to various aspects of his or her life

- light box (optional)

- five skeins of ultramarine-blue stranded embroidery thread

- circular embroidery frame

- fabric glue stick

- ultramarine-blue sewing thread

- ultramarine-blue quilting thread

- see also basic equipment (page 108)

to make the quilt

1 Cut two pieces measuring 192 x 145cm (75½ x 57in) from the gingham fabric. Cut the wadding to the same size. Lay one piece of gingham fabric on the floor wrong side up (if applicable), lay the wadding on top, and place the second piece of gingham fabric on top of that, right side up (if applicable). Pin-baste the entire quilt, avoiding the very edges, following the instructions on page 112.

2 Cut four binding strips from the length of the blue fabric as follows: two strips measuring 200 x 10cm (79 x 4in) long and two strips measuring 150 x 10cm (59 x 4in). Prepare each strip following the instructions on page 121.

3 Using ultramarine-blue sewing thread, bind the quilt following the instructions on page 122, short ends first.

4 Enlarge the drawings on a photocopier so that each image fits comfortably inside a rectangle from 18 x 12cm (7 x 4¾in) to 36 x 23cm (14¼ x 9in) with a comfortable border all round (✂ 4).

5 Take one of the photocopied drawings and put it on a light box if you have one. If not, tape it to a window. Cut a rectangle of white fabric to a suitable size, and trace the image onto the fabric using a water-soluble marker.

6 Put your work in a circular embroidery frame and embroider over the lines using three strands of ultramarine-blue embroidery thread and a small, neat backstitch (see page 115).

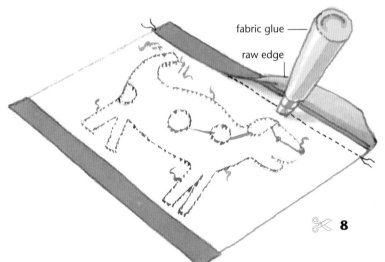

fabric glue

raw edge

✂ **8**

8 Press the binding to the wrong side along the centre fold and glue the binding in place on the reverse of the rectangle using a fabric glue stick (✂ 8). Repeat with the short sides, and all the other rectangles.

9 Lay the quilt on the floor, right side up. Arrange the embroidered pictures randomly on the quilt, at different angles, until you are happy with the arrangement. Remove any safety pins that are in the way and pin the pictures in place with quilting pins.

10 Machine the pictures in place, sewing down the middle of the binding and using blue quilting thread. You may find manoeuvring the quilt tricky, so sew just two sides of each picture at a time, cutting the thread and rotating the quilt to sew the other sides.

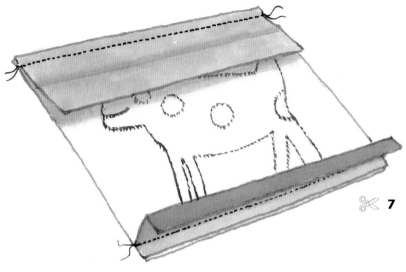

✂ **7**

7 Cut strips of the plain blue fabric 4cm (1½in) wide and join them to form one long strip, approximately 600cm (236in) in total. Take one of your embroidered rectangles and cut two strips the same length as the longer sides. Fold each strip in half lengthways and press in place. With right sides together, lay the strips along the long edges of the rectangle, with raw edges level. Machine-sew along the strips, taking a 1cm (⅜in) seam (✂ 7).

Alternatives

Use a variety of coloured threads for the images or embroider the pictures in black or dark grey and get your child to colour them in using fabric pens. Heat-set the colouring following the manufacturer's instructions.

Busy Weekend

These fun projects are the most detailed and require the widest range of skills. They are therefore not recommended for complete beginners.

Furthermore, some require a certain amount of preparatory work, in addition to the weekend needed to make the quilt up. However, if are organized and work in a methodical way, you should be able to get the bulk of the work completed in two days.

Alphabet Quilt

This quilt makes learning the alphabet child's play. There is an assortment of different typefaces to choose from, although you can use just one if you prefer. Make the patterns for the characters by printing them from a computer in a large font size or enlarge them from the templates on page 138.

This project uses a different technique for binding, which is quicker and simpler, although it needs wide-width fabric.

The finished size of the quilt is approximately 156 x 133cm (61½ x 52½in). You can also use the quilt as a playmat or wall hanging in a child's playroom.

✄ you will need

Fabric quantities assume a width of at least
110cm (43in) unless stated otherwise*
Seam allowance 1.5cm (⅝in)

- 210cm (83in) red fabric with widely spaced white dots for backing, binding and squares (*width at least 155cm (61in), or join two lengths of narrower fabric, see page 111)

- 30cm (12in) fine yellow-and-white check

- 30cm (12in) light-blue fabric with red dots

- 30cm (12in) white fabric with fine light-blue stripes

- 30cm (12in) green fabric with white dots

- 30cm (12in) yellow fabric

- 30cm (12in) light-blue fabric with white dots

- 30cm (12in) pink fabric with white dots

- 30cm (12in) yellow alphabet fabric

- 20cm (8in) red fabric with closely spaced white dots

- 20cm (8in) red fabric

- 30cm (12in) mid-blue fabric with fine blue dots

- 130cm (51in) blue alphabet fabric

- 130 x 46cm (51 x 18in) fusible webbing

- red, yellow, green, light blue, pink and mid-blue machine-embroidery threads

- neutral-coloured and red sewing threads

- 140 x 160cm (55 x 63in) 55g (2oz) polyester wadding (batting)

- invisible quilting thread

- see also basic equipment (page 108)

- thin card or acetate for the templates, cut as follows:
  21cm (8¼in) square
  18cm (7⅛in) square

to make the quilt

1 From the red fabric with widely spaced white dots, cut a piece 180cm (71in) long from the width of the fabric for the backing. Set to one side. You will be left with a strip 30cm (12in) deep. Using the 21cm (8¼in) square template, cut four squares from this strip and reserve the leftover piece of fabric for the letter 'U'.

2 Cut 21cm (8¼in) squares from the fabrics as follows (required number listed in brackets), reserving any leftovers for the letters):
• fine yellow-and-white check fabric (five)
• light-blue fabric with red dots (two)
• white fabric with fine light-blue stripes (four)
• green fabric with white dots (three)
• yellow fabric (two)
• light-blue fabric with white dots (three)
• pink fabric with white dots (three)
• yellow alphabet fabric (four)

3 Make your patterns for the letters, either by enlarging the templates on pages 139–141 or by printing out your own 475pt letters on a computer. (Set the computer to print on the 'outline' setting to save ink.) Use the printed or enlarged letters as your patterns.

4 Cut the fusible webbing into 15cm (6in) squares – one for each letter. Iron the webbing onto the back of the fabrics as follows:
• red fabric with closely spaced white dots: letters A and R
• yellow fabric: letters B, I, M and Z
• green fabric with white dots: letters C, J and Y
• pink fabric with white dots: letters D and P
• white fabric with fine light-blue stripes: letters E and Q
• light-blue fabric with white dots: letters F, O and V
• red fabric: letters G, K, S and X
• mid-blue fabric with fine blue dots: letters H, L, N, T and W
• red fabric with widely spaced white dots: letter U

5 Using the patterns, cut out each letter and centre on its appropriate square. Bond in place following the manufacturer's instructions. If you wish, machine-sew satin stitch around each letter using a matching colour of machine-embroidery thread.

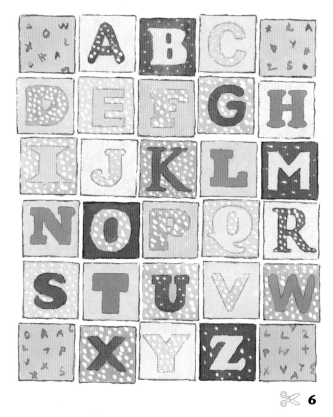

✂ **6**

6 Arrange the squares in rows (✂ 6), and pin in each row together following the instructions on page 110. For accuracy, mark the seam allowance on the back of each square using the 18cm (7⅛in) square template and a vanishing marker. Machine-stitch the squares together using a neutral-coloured thread, and press the seams open.

7 Join the rows together, ensuring the seams align (see page 111). Press the seams open.

r.s.

wadding

backing fabric

12a

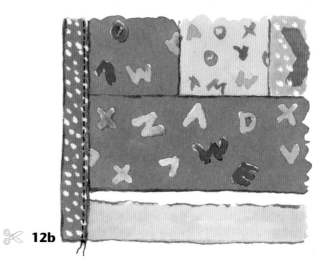

12b

8 From the full length of the blue alphabet fabric, cut four border strips, 21cm (8¼in) wide. With right sides facing and raw edges level, pin and sew one strip to either side of the alphabet panel. Press the seams open and trim the ends of the strip level with the top and bottom of the panel. Take the other two strips and sew one to the top and one to the bottom of the panel in the same way, trimming the ends level with the edges of the first two border strips (✂ 8).

9 Use the quilt top to cut the wadding 1.5cm (⅝in) larger all round.

10 Using invisible thread in the top of your machine and red thread in the bobbin, quilt along all seam lines by stitching-in-the-ditch (see page 112).

11 Centre the quilt top and the wadding on the reserved backing fabric, and cut the fabric 8cm (3⅛in) larger all round than the wadding.

12 Starting at the sides, fold the extended part of the red fabric in half along its length (✂ 12a), then fold again, onto the front of the quilt, and pin to form a 4cm (1½in) binding strip. Machine-sew the binding in place on the front of the quilt, 5mm (³⁄₁₆in) from the edge of the border, using red sewing thread (✂ 12b).

13 Repeat on the short ends and oversew the corners with red sewing thread (see page 117).

Wild West Quilt

This cot quilt has a cowboy feel to it, with squares of lightweight denim, gingham and shirting fabrics, contrasting bold red stars and rustic top stitching. The mix of fabric used in the quilt suggests it is made out of scraps, in keeping with the pioneering tradition of American quilts. If you prefer, you can use just two background fabrics – white and denim, for example – for a bolder effect, with just one red fabric for the stars.

The finished size of the quilt is approximately 130 x 100cm (51 x 39in), allowing sufficient tuck-in for a standard cot mattress. You can scale up the quilt to fit a larger cot or a single bed or mount it as a wall hanging.

✂ you will need

Fabric quantities assume a width of at least 115 cm (45in)

For the light squares:
- 20cm (8in) fine blue-and-white stripes
- 20cm (8in) lilac-and-turquoise check
- 40cm (16in) white fabric
- 20cm (8in) fine grey-and-white check

For the dark squares:
- 20cm (8in) lightweight denim
- 20cm (8in) navy-and-white small gingham
- 20cm (8in) fine turquoise-and-cream stripes
- 20cm (8in) dark denim
- 20cm (8in) printed denim-effect fabric
- 200cm (79in) larger scale red gingham check for backing and binding strips

For the stars:
- 20cm (8in) small red gingham
- 20cm (8in) red with small white dots
- 20cm (8in) red-and-green check
- 20cm (8in) red
- 122 x 44cm (48 x 17¼in) fusible webbing
- white and red embroidery threads
- light-blue and white sewing threads
- invisible quilting thread
- 100 x 130cm (39 x 51in) 55g (2oz) polyester wadding (batting)
- see also basic equipment (page 108)
- thin card or acetate for templates, cut as follows:
  19cm (7½in) square
  16cm (6¼in) square
  star (see page 138)
  star positioning guide (see page 138)

to make the quilt

1 Using the 19cm (7½in) square template, cut the fabrics as follows (required number of squares in brackets):
- blue-and-white stripes fabric (five)
- lilac-and-turquoise check fabric (five)
- white fabric (ten)
- fine grey-and-white check fabric (four)
- lightweight denim fabric (six)
- navy-and-white small gingham fabric (five)
- fine turquoise-and-cream stripes fabric (six)
- dark denim fabric (three)
- printed denim-effect fabric (four)

2 Cut the fusible webbing to fit your various pieces of red fabric and iron onto the back of each, following the webbing manufacturer's instructions. Using the star template, draw the correct number of stars onto the backing paper of each fabric, in rows, with their points almost touching. You should be able to fit eight into a full row. Cut the stars out carefully.

3 Place the star positioning guide exactly over each light-coloured square. Remove the paper backing of the fusible webbing and lay the star in the centre of the guide. Remove the positioning guide and iron the star in place following the webbing manufacturer's instructions. Repeat with all the stars.

4 Draw guidelines 3mm (⅛in) from the outer and inner edges of each star, using a ruler and a vanishing marker. Sew along the lines by hand in small, neat running stitches, using three strands of red embroidery thread for the outer edges and three strands of white or red thread for the inner edges. Press the embroidery on the wrong side using a medium iron and a damp cloth.

✂ **5**

5 Following the arrangement we have used (✂ 5) lay the squares out in six rows of eight, ensuring that all the stars are the same way up, with a point directed vertically towards the top of the quilt. Follow the instructions on page 110 to join the squares in each row taking 1.5cm (⅝in) seams and using a light-blue sewing thread. For accuracy, draw seam lines on the back using the 16cm (6¼in) square and a vanishing marker. Machine-sew, then press the seams open. Mark the row number on each left-hand square.

6 Join the rows in the same way, laying them out, one above the other on your work surface (✂ 6). Again, ensure that all the stars are the right way up. Pin each strip to its

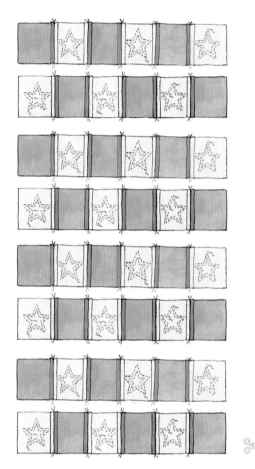

✄ **6**

neighbour along the seam line. Machine-sew the strips together and press all seams open.

7 Take the larger-scale red gingham check and, following the cutting guide (✄ 7), cut six binding strips. Join two of the long strips to the two short strips, end-to-end, and press the seams open.

8 Use the quilt top as a template to cut the remaining red gingham fabric 3cms (1¼in) wider all round. This is the backing fabric. Cut the wadding to the same size. Pin-baste through all three layers (see instructions on page 112).

9 Using invisible quilting thread in the top of your machine and white thread in the bobbin, machine-quilt along all long seams by stitching-in-the-ditch (see page 112).

10 Prepare the binding strips following the instructions on page 121.

11 Bind the quilt, starting with the shorter ends, and following the instructions on page 122.

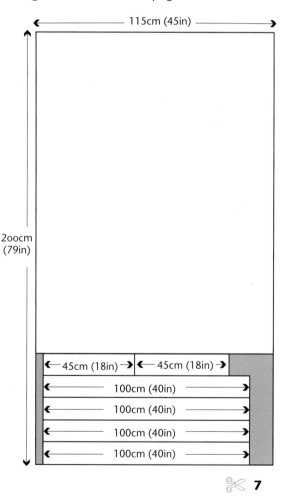

✄ **7**

Friendship Quilt

Also known as an album quilt, a friendship quilt results from the joint efforts of various friends and family members. Once made, therefore, it is bound to become something of an heirloom. Each person involved makes up one or more squares for the quilt, and it is your job to assemble the quilt, adding fabric sashes between the squares. While the quilt cannot be produced from scratch in a weekend, it can certainly be assembled in this time.

The finished size of the quilt is approximately 178 x 130cm (70 x 51in), which is fine for a topper for a single bed. You can also make the quilt into a wall hanging.

✂ you will need

Fabric quantities assume a width of at least 110cm (43in) unless stated otherwise*
Seam allowance 1.5cm (⅝in)

- 100cm (39in) off-white or cream fabric

- 25cm (10in) apple-green fabric

- 25cm (10in) orange fabric

- 25cm (10in) duck-egg fabric

- 25cm (10in) light-green fabric

- 25cm (10in) orange-red fabric

- 25cm (10in) soft-yellow fabric

- 160cm (63in) taupe-and-white gingham check fabric for sashes

- 40cm (16in) taupe fabric for sash squares

- 100cm (39in) taupe-and-red check for the binding

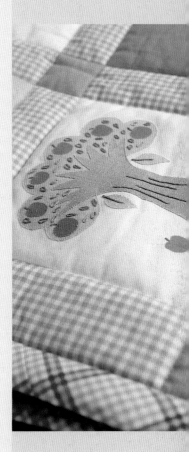

- 180cm (71cm) wide-width* (at least 130cm (51in)) taupe-and-cream large check or plain cream fabric for backing

- assortment of muted plain and simple printed fabrics for appliqué and piecing

- off-white or cream sewing thread

- invisible quilting thread

- 180 x 135cm (71 x 53in) 55g (2oz) or 115g (4oz) polyester wadding (batting)

- see also basic equipment (page 108)

- thin card for the templates, cut as follows:
  22cm (8¾in) square
  22 x 8cm (8¾in x 3³⁄₁₆in) rectangle
  8cm (3³⁄₁₆in) square

Note Ask contributors not to use beads, buttons or anything else likely to cause a choking hazard, especially if the quilt is for a child under three years old. Ensure all appliqué pieces are securely fixed in place.

to make the quilt

1 Ask friends and family members to make a square or squares for your quilt, giving them suggestions and fabric samples as a guide to the sorts of colours you would like them to use. It makes sense to have an overall colour scheme and an idea of what each person intends to do before they start. Suitable techniques include patchwork piecing (log cabin, pinwheel, nine-patch), appliqué, embroidery, drawing with fabric pens, painting and printing with fabric paints and stencilling.

Motifs can include anything, although simple shapes often work best: a balloon; a heart; the sun or moon; birth signs; leaves or flowers; animals such as a butterfly, cat, dog, or fish; birds such as an owl, duck, or cockerel; fruit such as an apple, pear, or cherries. Abstract patterns can also work well.

2 Once you have the ideas, you can send specific materials to your friends and relatives so they can complete their square(s). You will need to cut eighteen 22cm (8¾in) squares from the off-white or cream fabric for the album squares. (Note that the four corner squares in this quilt are pieced and you will need larger amounts of cream fabric if you intend to include any in your quilt, depending on the type of piecing).

3 From each of the plain-coloured fabrics, cut three 22cm (8¾in) squares, except the apple green, from which you cut two squares. From the taupe gingham, using the 22 x 8cm (8¾ x 3³⁄₁₆in) rectangular template, cut 42 vertical and 40 horizontal sashes. (Be sure to cut them vertically and horizontally, because the weave of gingham checks can vary slightly). Using the 8cm (3³⁄₁₆in) square cut 48 sashes from the plain taupe fabric.

✄ **4**

4 Once your friends and family have returned all the album squares to you, lay them out on the floor in a pleasing arrangement, alternating them with plain-coloured squares and placing any pieced squares at the corners. Position the vertical and horizontal sashes between each square, and place a taupe sash square at each intersection (✄ 4).

5 Following the instructions on page 110, and using off-white or cream sewing thread, join the patches in each vertical row, starting with a row of sashes. Join the rows together in the same way, ensuring the seams align.

6 Use the quilt top to cut the backing fabric 1cm (⅜in) wider all round. Cut the wadding to the same size as the backing. Lay the backing on the floor wrong side up (if applicable), lay the wadding on top and centre the quilt top on that. There should be an even border of wadding all round. Pin-baste through all three layers, avoiding the seam lines, and following the instructions on page 112.

7 Using invisible thread in the top of your machine and off-white or cream thread in the bobbin, quilt along all seam lines by stitching-in-the-ditch (see page 112).

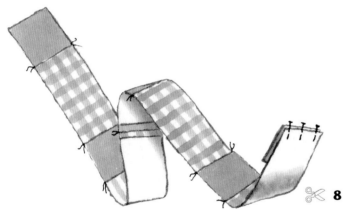

8 Cut 9cm (3½in) wide bias strips from the taupe-and-red check fabric. Join the strips to form a piece approximately 640cm (250in) long (✂ 8). Cut two 182cm (71½in) strips and two 138cm (54in) strips. Prepare each strip following the instructions on page 121.

9 Use off-white or cream thread to bind the edges of the quilt, beginning with the long sides, and following the instructions on page 122.

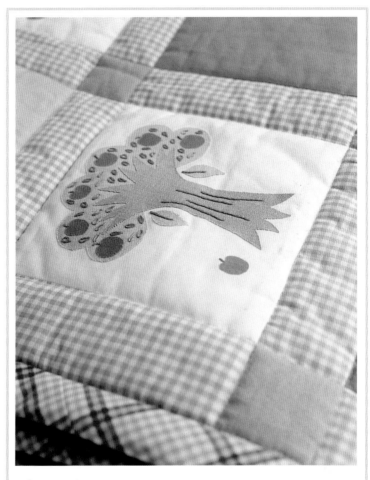

Alternatives

You could ask the makers to produce all the squares using the same technique, such as embroidery or appliqué, or to use just one colour and white, such as blue and white or red and white. Another option is to ask each maker to sign his or her square(s) using an indelible fabric pen.

Sunny Sawtooth Quilt

Sawtooth is a traditional patchwork pattern that forms zigzag lines across the quilt. Here, triangles of marbled plains coordinate with children's novelty prints to form coloured squares and create the traditional zigzag effect. This is a great quilt to make from scraps and offcuts and, while it may look complicated, it uses a short cut that means each square is made in half the time.

The finished size of the quilt is approximately 169 x 143cm (66½ x 56¼in) wide, which will fit a standard cot. Alternatively you can use the quilt as a wall hanging or scale it up to fit a single bed.

✂ you will need

Fabric quantities assume a width of at least 110cm (43in)
Seam allowance 1.5cm (⅝in)

- 190cm (75in) red marbled fabric (includes backing fabric)

- 40cm (16in) pink marbled fabric

- 40cm (16in) green marbled fabric

- 40cm (16in) light-blue marbled fabric

- 40cm (16in) yellow marbled fabric

- 40cm (16in) violet marbled fabric

- 40cm (16in) red patterned fabric

- 40cm (16in) yellow patterned fabric

- 40cm (16in) violet patterned fabric

- 40cm (16in) pink patterned fabric

- 40cm (16in) green patterned fabric

- 40cm (16in) light-blue patterned fabric

- 60cm (24in) green printed fabric for binding

- 150 x 120cm (59 x 47in) 55g (2oz) polyester wadding (batting)

- neutral-coloured sewing thread

- invisible quilting thread

- see also basic equipment (page 108)

- acetate for the templates, cut as follows:
  16.5cm (6½in) square
  11.3cm (4⁹⁄₁₆in) square
  seam guide for sawtooth square
  (see page 138)

to make the quilt

1 Using the 16.5cm (6½in) square template, cut squares of the marbled fabric as follows: eleven red, nine pink, nine green, nine light blue, eight yellow and eight violet.

2 Using the 16.5cm (6½in) square template, cut squares of fabric as follows (required number of listed in brackets):
- red pattern fabric (eleven)
- yellow pattern fabric (eight)
- violet pattern fabric (eight)
- pink pattern fabric (nine)
- green pattern fabric (nine)
- light-blue pattern fabric (nine)

sewing lines

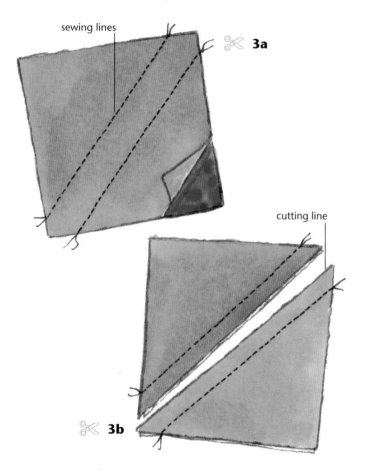

3a

cutting line

3b

3 Using the seam guide template, draw two diagonal lines on the back of each marbled square using a vanishing marker or a light pencil. Pair up the marbled fabrics with their coordinating prints and pin together right sides facing, keeping the pins away from the diagonal lines. Machine-sew along the two diagonal lines on each pair of squares using a neutral-coloured sewing thread (✂ 3a). Chain the squares as you sew them (see page 111). Trim the squares apart, then cut each square from corner to corner between the rows of stitching (✂ 3b). Press the seams open. You will now have two squares, each with one diagonal of marbled fabric and the other of printed fabric.

4 Arrange the squares randomly in twelve rows of nine squares. Take every alternate square and centre the 11.3cm (4⁹⁄₁₆in) square template on the back. Draw around it with a vanishing marker or light pencil line to give you an accurate sewing line.

5 Following the instructions on page 111, pin together the squares in each row, ensuring each square is the correct way round, and machine-stitch together (✂ 5). Press the seams open, and mark the row number on each left-hand square.

✂ **5**

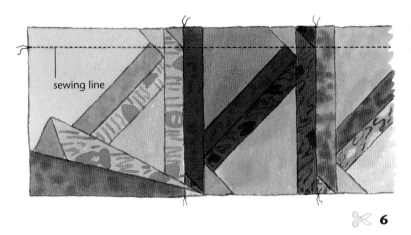

sewing line

✂ **6**

6 Join the rows together in the same way, ensuring they are in the correct order. As you sew, make sure you stitch across each seam where the point of the small triangle in the seam allowance meets the vertical seam (✂ 6). Press the seams open.

7 Use the quilt top as a template to cut the backing fabric 3cm (1⅛in) bigger all round. Cut a piece of wadding to the same size as the backing fabric. Lay the backing fabric on the floor wrong side up (if applicable), lay the wadding on top, then centre the quilt top on that. There should be an even border of wadding showing all round. Pin-baste the whole quilt, avoiding the seams, and following the instructions on page 112.

8 Using invisible quilting thread in the top of your machine and a neutral-coloured thread in the bobbin, quilt along all seam lines by stitching-in-the-ditch (see page 112).

9 Cut five binding strips 11cm (4⅜in) deep from the width of the binding fabric. Cut one binding strip into two equal lengths and sew each piece, end-to-end, onto another binding strip. Press the seams open. You now have two shorter and two longer pieces.

10 Prepare the binding strips following the instructions on page 121.

11 Using a neutral-coloured thread, and following the instructions on page 122, bind the quilt, starting with the longer sides.

Alternatives
Choose other novelty fabrics, or use just one printed and one plain fabric to make the sawtooth squares.

Night-time Cushion

The smiling moon on this large, crazy patchwork cushion is friendly and sleepy, making it perfect for a child's bedroom. Although it may appear complicated, crazy patchwork is actually very simple to do. The joins are over sewn with fancy embroidery, which helps to strengthen them and softens the transition between fabrics. If you don't have a sewing machine that can do embroidery, you can either use machine zigzag or hand-embroider the stitches.

The finished size of the cushion is approximately 65cm (25½in) square. You can also convert the front panel into a wall hanging.

✂ you will need

Fabric quantities assume a width of at least
 110cm (43in)
Seam allowance 1.5cm (⅝in)

- 60cm (24in) black fabric with stars and
  moons for patchwork and binding

- assortment of fat quarters and offcuts of
  about ten star and moon fabrics with black,
  navy and blue backgrounds

- 15 x 10cm (6 x 4in) offcut of light-grey
  crackle-effect fabric for moon

- 70cm (28in) navy-and-gold flecked fabric for
  the cushion back

- 15 x 10cm (6 x 4in) fusible webbing

- blue sewing thread

- off-white and yellow shaded machine-
  embroidery threads

(or stranded embroidery threads for hand-
embroidery)

- mid-grey and bright-red stranded
  embroidery threads

- 65cm (25½in) square cushion pad or pillow

- 55cm (21½in) lightweight navy zip

- approx. 300cm (118in) no. 4 cotton piping
  cord

- see also basic equipment (page 108)

- thin paper for the pattern, cut as follows:
  68cm (26¾in) square

- thin paper for the templates (pages 134–135)

Note This cushion must not be used as a
pillow for sleeping on, nor given to babies
under one year old.

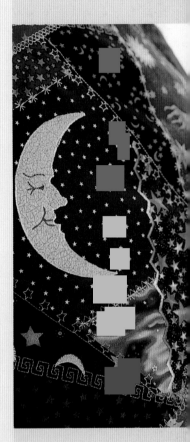

91

to make the cushion cover

1 From the fabric you have chosen for the binding, make 5cm (2in) wide bias strips following the instructions on page 121. Join where necessary with blue sewing thread to form a 280cm (110in) continuous strip. Set to one side and use the remnants of the fabric for the crazy patchwork.

2 Trace the templates onto the thin paper. Using one of the plainer, darker fabrics with a small-scale design (to give a good contrast with the moon motif) cut the six-sided central shape. Reverse the moon motif and trace onto the paper backing of the fusible webbing. Iron onto the wrong side of the grey crackle print, following the webbing manufacturer's instructions.

3 Cut out the motif using small, sharp scissors. Peel off the backing paper and iron the motif in the correct position on the central shape. Machine-stitch around the edge of the moon using off-white machine thread and satin stitch, then backstitch the eye in grey stranded embroidery thread and the mouth in bright red.

4 Cut pieces (A) and (B) (see page 134) from two further fabrics. With right sides and raw edges together, pin to either end of the central shape. Machine-sew in place, using blue sewing thread, and taking a 1.5cm (⅝in) seam (✂ 4). Press the seams open, then embroider on the right side along the seam lines using a machine-embroidery stitch or suitable hand-embroidery stitch (see page 115) and yellow thread.

5 Cut pieces (C) and (D) (see page 135) from two further fabrics and attach to either side of the shape in the same way (✂ 5). Press the seams open, and embroider over the seam lines. Press the embroidery with a damp cloth.

A

B

D

C

✂ **5**

6 Continue to add further pieces of fabric to the edges of the panel, lining up the straight edges of the patches with the straight edges of the centre panel. Use larger pieces of fabric than you think you need and trim them to line up with surrounding patches (✂ 6). Each time, embroider along the seam line as before.

A

D

✂ **6**

C

B

7 Build up the cushion in this way until the project is larger than 68cm (26¾in) square all round. Trim carefully to 68cm (26¾in) square, ensuring the moon is lying on its back. If you make a paper pattern to this size you will find trimming much easier. Round off the corners by placing a saucer on the corners and using it as a template.

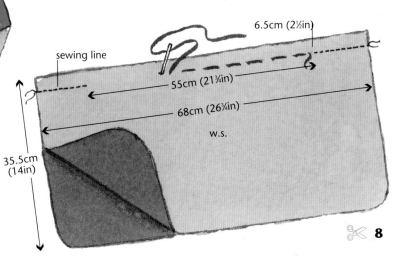

6.5cm (2½in)

sewing line

55cm (21¾in)

68cm (26¾in)

w.s.

35.5cm (14in)

✂ **8**

8 Cut two pieces from the backing fabric, measuring 68 x 35.5cm (26¾ x 14in). Place the two halves on top of each other, right sides together and round off two corners on one long side using the paper template from step 5. Stitch along the seam line on the long, non-rounded edge, 6.5cm (2½in) from the top and bottom edges, leaving a 55cm (21¾in) gap. Tack the rest of the opening shut (✂ 8) and press the seams open.

9 Knot the ends of the piping cord to prevent them unravelling and wash in hot water to pre-shrink it. Then take the strips of binding and follow the instructions on page 128 to complete the cushion.

Floral Quilt

The finished size of the quilt is 192 x 143cm (75½in x 56¼in).

This single-bed sized quilt will delight older girls. The design of the quilt, known as 'diamond-in-square', is traditional and timeless. Despite being a mix of patterns, the ten fabrics coordinate beautifully because each has a similar range of sugared-almond colours.

✂ you will need

Fabric quantities assume a width of at least 150cm (59in)

- 50cm (20in) pink paisley fabric

- 50cm (20in) blue floral fabric

- 50cm (20in) white floral fabric

- 30cm (12in) blue paisley fabric

- 250cm (100in) blue-and-red spotted fabric

- 100cm (39in) green, white and red check fabric

- 60cm (24in) blue, red and pink check fabric

- 40cm (16in) pink-and-red spotted fabric

- 40cm (16in) green-and-red spotted fabric

- 60cm (24in) buff-and-red spotted fabric

- 200 x 145cm (79 x 57in) 55g (2oz) polyester wadding (batting)

- rotary cutter and cutting mat (see page 109)

- neutral-coloured and light-blue sewing threads

- invisible quilting thread

- see also basic equipment (page 108)

- thin card or acetate for making templates, cut as follows:
  24cm (9⁷⁄₁₆in) square
  20cm (7⅞in) square
  17cm (6¾in) square
  16.5cm (6½in) square

to make the quilt

1 Using the 20cm (7⅞in) square template cut the fabric as follows (required squares listed in brackets):
- pink paisley fabric (twelve)
- blue floral fabric (eight)
- white floral fabric (nine)
- blue paisley fabric (six)

Using the 16.5cm (6½in) square template cut the fabric as follows:
- blue, red and pink check fabric (eighteen)
- pink-and-red spotted fabric (twelve)

Follow the cutting guides for the remaining fabrics:
- blue-and-red spotted fabric (✂ 1a)
- green, white and red check fabric (✂ 1b)
- green-and-red spotted fabric (✂ 1c)
- buff-and-red spotted fabric (✂ 1d)

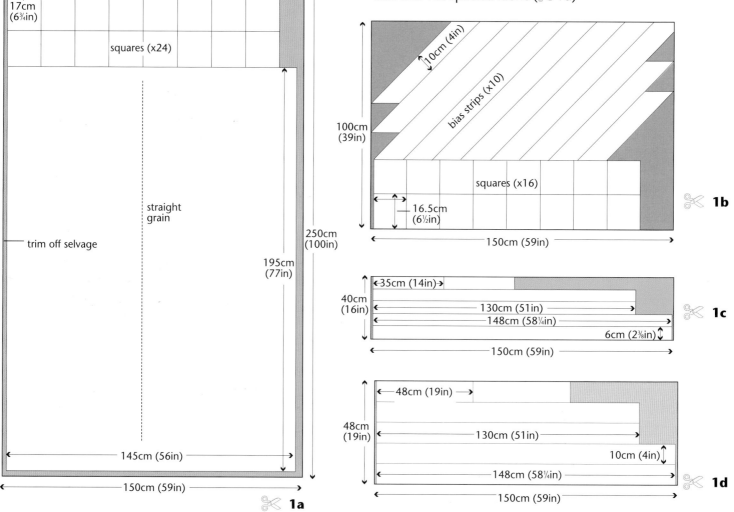

17cm (6¾in)

squares (x24)

straight grain

trim off selvage

250cm (100in)

195cm (77in)

145cm (56in)

150cm (59in)

✂ **1a**

10cm (4in)

bias strips (x10)

100cm (39in)

squares (x16)

16.5cm (6½in)

150cm (59in)

✂ **1b**

35cm (14in)

40cm (16in)

130cm (51in)

148cm (58¼in)

6cm (2⅜in)

150cm (59in)

✂ **1c**

48cm (19in)

48cm (19in)

130cm (51in)

10cm (4in)

148cm (58¼in)

150cm (59in)

✂ **1d**

2 Cut all the 16.5cm (6½in) squares in half diagonally using a rotary cutter (see page 109) and place in three piles, one for each fabric design.

3 Centre the 17cm (6¾in) square template on the wrong side of each 20cm (7⅞in) fabric square and draw round it with erasable pen to mark the seam allowance. The seam allowance should be of equal width on all sides of the square, and should measure 1.5cm (⅝in) wide.

4 Create four piles of shapes:
    Pile one: pink paisley fabric and blue-and-red spotted fabric
    Pile two: blue floral fabric and green, white and red check fabric
    Pile three: white floral fabric and blue, red and pink check fabric
    Pile four: blue paisley fabric and pink-and-red spotted fabric

5 Begin with pile one. Place a triangle on your work surface, right side up and with the long edge at the top. Take a 20cm (7⅞in) square of fabric and lay it, wrong side up, on top of the triangle so that one edge of the square lines up with the long edge of the triangle, with equal amounts of the triangle projecting on either side beyond the square. The right sides of both pieces of fabric will be together (✂ 5).

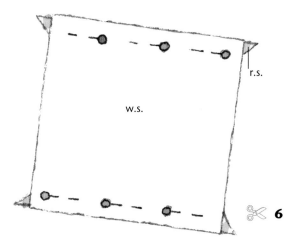

6 Pin along the seam line so the sharp ends of the pins point to the left. Turn the square right round through 180 degrees. Take a second triangle and repeat step 5 (✂ 6). Do this with all the squares in each pile.

7 Take each square in turn and, using a neutral-coloured sewing thread, machine-sew along one seam, with the pins on the top surface of the fabric and the bulk of the fabric to your left. The pins should have their heads towards you for easy removal as you sew along the marked seam line. Without cutting the thread (known as 'chaining', see page 111), take another square and sew this in the same way, leaving a gap of between 1–2cms (½–1in) between the pieces. Continue like this until you have sewn each square in the pile along one seam.

8 Cut the thread between the squares and stack them back in their piles. Starting again, take each square in turn and machine-sew the second seam. Complete each pile of squares before you start the next, until you have sewn both seams on all squares.

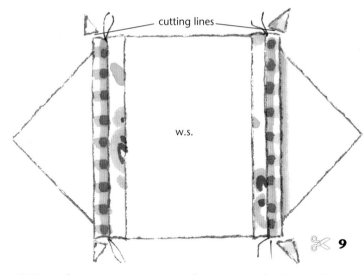

cutting lines

w.s.

✂ **9**

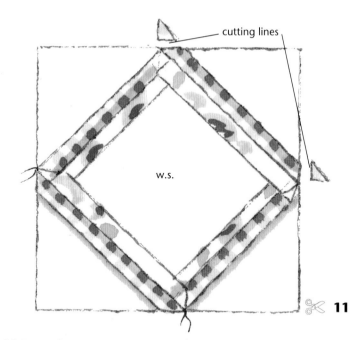

cutting lines

w.s.

✂ **11**

9 Press the seams open on each square and snip the four projecting points level (✂ 9). Do this to all the squares in each pile.

10 Take a square from pile one, now with two attached triangles, and position it on your work surface wrong side up. Turn the square so the triangles are to the left and right. Repeat steps 5 to 9 with two new triangles each time, until you have sewn all the squares.

11 Press the seams open on each square and snip off the projecting points level with the edge of the larger square you have created (✂ 11).

12 Place the 24cm (9⁷⁄₁₆in) square template on the wrong side of each large square and repeat the instructions in step 3.

13 Take three squares from pile one (1) and two squares from pile two (2). Arrange them on your work surface in a row in the order 1-2-1-2-1, then pin them together, wrong sides facing, to form a strip. Repeat three more times until you have used up all the squares in piles one and two. Sew the seams and press all the seams open.

14 Take three squares from pile three (3) and two squares from pile four (4). Pin them together, following the same instructions as for step 13, except the order will now be 3-4-3-4-3. Repeat this whole step twice more until you have used up all the squares in piles three and four. Machine-sew along each pinned seam, and press the seams open.

✂ **15**

17 With right sides facing, pin the shorter strips to the shorter ends of the quilt – they will extend beyond the quilt on either side. Machine-sew along the seam lines and press the seams open. Trim the strip level with the long edges of the quilt.

18 Take the two longer strips and pin them to the longer sides of the quilt. As in step 17, the strip will extend beyond the quilt on either side. Machine-sew along the seam lines and press the seams open. Trim the strip level with the strips you sewed on in step 17.

19 Take the buff-and-red spotted fabric strips and join the two 148cm (58¼in) strips to the 48cm (19in) strips. Press all seams open. Repeat steps 17 and 18, using these strips.

20 Lay the blue-and-red spotted backing piece on the floor wrong side up and lay your wadding neatly on top of it, smoothing out any bumps. Now lay the completed quilt top of the wadding, right side up. Trim the wadding and the backing so they are 3cm (1⅛in) wider all round than the top. Pin-baste the quilt through all layers, avoiding the vertical and horizontal seams, and following the instructions on page 112.

21 Using invisible quilting thread in the top of your machine and light-blue thread in the bobbin, stitch-in-the-ditch along the long seams in the centre panel, beginning and ending where the seam meets the first green border (see page 112). Quilt the short seams in the same way. This amount of quilting is adequate to hold the wadding in place, but if you have time to do more, you can quilt along the diagonals and the outer edges of the green strips.

22 Following the instructions on page 121, use the binding strips to make two 200cm (79in) long strips and two 150cm (59in) long strips. Bind the edges of the quilt, beginning with the short ends, and following the instructions on page 122.

15 Lay out the seven strips, right side up, one above the other so that the first strip starts with 1, the second strip with 3, the next strip 1, the next 3 and so on. The last strip should begin with 1 (✂ 15). Now pin each strip to its neighbour, along the seam line, and following the instructions on page 111. Ensure you match up the seams in each row, and that the points of the diamonds just touch when the seam is opened out. Machine-sew the strips together using a neutral-coloured sewing thread, and press all seams open.

16 Take the six strips you cut from the green-and-red spotted fabric and join the two 148cm (58¼in) strips, end-to-end to the 35cm (14in) strips. You should now have four strips, two shorter and two longer.

Windy-day Wall Hanging

As a refreshing alternative to a conventional framed picture on the wall, this cheerful wall hanging with its windy-day theme will definitely be popular with children. The images are bonded onto a pieced background, so the appliqué is quick and easy to do once you have cut out the shapes. It is a great way to use up scraps and offcuts of fabric, and you can use whatever colours you have available.

The finished size of the wall hanging is approximately 68cm (27in) square. You can make it larger if you wish.

✂ you will need

Seam allowance 1.5cm (⅝in)
For the background (the following are exact measurements – height then width):

- blue-and-white spotted fabric: 8cm (3⅛in) square

- blue marbled fabric: 18.5 x 8cm (7¼ x 3⅛in) and 23.5 x 5.5cm (9¼ x 2⅜in)

- blue-and-white striped fabric : 23.5 x 15cm (9¼ x 5⅞in) and 23.5 x 17.5cm (9¼ x 6⅞in)

- blue chambray fabric: 23.5 x 20cm (9¼ x 7⅞in)

- fine jade-and-white check print: 6 x 54cm (2⅜ x 21¼in)

- turquoise marbled fabric: 8cm (3⅛in) square

- jade-green fabric: 8 x 49cm (3⅛ x 19⁵⁄₁₆in)

- green-and-white spotted fabric: 11 x 5.5cm (4⁵⁄₁₆ x 2⅜in)

- apple-green fabric: 11 x 49cm (4⁵⁄₁₆ x 19⁵⁄₁₆in)

- lime-green and green striped fabric: 12cm by 5.5cm (4¾ x 2⅜in)

- lime-green and white small gingham check: 12 x 21cm (4¾ x 8¼in)

- plain lime-green fabric: 12 x 31cm (4¾ x 12³⁄₁₆in)

- small white-and-yellow printed check: three 8cm (3⅛in) squares

- small yellow-and-white gingham fabric: 8 x 15cm (3⅛ x 5⅞in)

- primrose-yellow fabric: 8 x 15cm (3⅛ x 5⅞in)

- bright-yellow fabric: 8 x 15cm (3⅛ x 5⅞in) and 5cm (2in) square

For the appliqué shapes:
- 20 x 15cm (7⅞ x 5⅞in) rectangle leaf-effect fabric

- 10cm (4in) square reddish-brown fabric

- 10cm (4in) square orange fabric

- 10cm (4in) square yellow-and-orange striped fabric

- remnants of bright-red fabric – (see page 102)

- 10cm (4in) square blue fabric with small white dots

- 12cm (4¾in) square blue fabric

- 10cm (4in) square golden-brown marbled fabric

(continued overleaf)

- 12cm (4¾in) square black fabric

- 7cm (2¾in) square pink fabric with red dots

- 7cm (2¾in) square pale yellow-pink ('flesh white') fabric

- 10cm (4in) square pale-brown fabric

- 10cm (4in) square black-and-cream tiny check fabric

- 10 x 12cm (4 x 4¾in) blue-and-white floral fabric

- 50cm (20in) bright-red fabric for the borders (70cm (28in) wide minimum)

- 80cm (32in) white fabric for backing (70cm (28in) wide minimum)

- 25cm (10in) brown fabric with white dots for the binding (70cm (28in) wide minimum)

- 50cm (20in) fusible webbing

- neutral and white sewing threads

- bright-red, bright-orange, black and grass-green stranded embroidery threads

- dark-green, black and red fabric marker pens

- 70cm (28cm) square cotton wadding (batting)

- 60cm (24in) length medium dowelling

- two self-adhesive plastic hooks

- see also basic equipment (page 108)

- thin card or paper for the templates on pages 136–137

to make the wall hanging

1 Arrange the background shapes and according to the diagram (✂ 1). Following the instructions on page 110, sew the pieces in one row at a time, then join the rows (see page 111) to form a square using a neutral-coloured sewing thread.

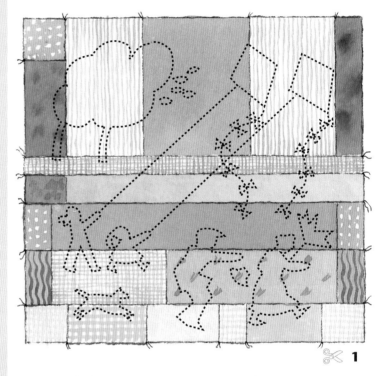

✂ **1**

2 Trace off the templates for the appliqué and transfer to the backing paper of the fusible webbing. Cut the shapes from the fabrics as follows:
- bright yellow fabric (girl's hair)
- leaf-effect fabric (tree foliage)
- reddish-brown fabric (tree trunks)
- orange fabric (kite triangles and three kite tail bows)
- yellow-and-orange striped fabric (kite triangles and three kite tail bows)
- bright-red fabric (kite triangles, three kite tail bows, boy's top and girl's shoes)
- blue fabric with small white dots (kite triangles,

three kite tail bows and boy's scarf)
- blue fabric (woman's hat, sleeves and shoes, and boy's trousers)
- golden-brown marbled fabric (boy's face, hands and ankles, woman's hair and legs, and dog's collar)
- black fabric (umbrella, dog, boy's hair and shoes, and man's hair, hat and shoes)
- pink fabric with red dots (girl's dress)
- pale yellow-pink fabric (woman's face and hands, girl's face, hands and legs, and man's face and hands)
- pale-brown fabric (man's coat)
- black-and-cream tiny check fabric (man's trousers – in three parts)
- blue-and-white floral fabric (woman's dress)

3 Position the appliqué shapes in their correct positions on the background and iron in place.

4 Draw the lines for the kite strings and tails with a vanishing marker. Using two strands of black embroidery thread, sew the kite strings in a small, neat running stitch. Using three strands of orange embroidery thread, chain-stitch the left-hand kite string, and using three strands of red embroidery thread, chain-stitch the right-hand kite string. Using three strands of green embroidery thread, embroider the grass blades in stem stitch (see page 115 for embroidery stitches).

5 From the width of the red border fabric, cut two strips measuring 66.5 x 10cm (26 x 4in) and two strips 54 x 9.5cm (21 x 3¾in). Sew the shorter border pieces along the top and bottom of the square panel, then sew the longer pieces to the sides. Press all seams open.

6 Using the appliqué panel as a template, cut the backing fabric to the same size, and cut a strip of fabric for the sleeve 55 x 7cm (22 x 3in). Turn the short ends of the sleeve in 1.5cm (⅝in) and machine in place with white sewing thread. Fold both long raw edges under 1.5cm. Attach the sleeve to the backing fabric.

7 Cut the wadding to the same size as the backing fabric. Lay the backing fabric down, wrong side up, then the wadding on top and the appliqué panel on top, right side up. Pin-baste through all layers, avoiding the join between the border and the central panel, and following the instructions on page 112.

8 Stitch-in-the-ditch along these seams (see page 112), using invisible quilting thread in the top of your machine and white sewing thread in the bobbin.

9 From the brown fabric with white dots cut four strips for the binding, each 70 x 5cm (27½ x 2in) and prepare each one following the instructions on page 121.

10 Bind the picture, starting with the top and bottom edges, and following the instructions on page 122. Insert the dowelling into the sleeve and hang with two hooks.

Alternatives
Use it as the central panel for a cushion cover (see page 128).

Materials, Equipment & Techniques

This section contains a summary of the equipment, techniques, materials and skills needed to complete the projects. There are cross-references within the projects to pages in this section. and, even if you are an experienced quilter, you may find it useful to scan through these pages before starting a project.

Materials

Quilting materials are widely available from department stores, fabric shops, specialist craft shops, by mail order and on the Internet. If your work is to look good, be durable and comfortable to use, it is important that you use the most appropriate materials for each project.

Fabric

The quilter's favourite is one hundred per cent cotton. This is the easiest to work with and presses well. For the best results, use a similar weight and finish of fabric for all of the pieces in any one project. A mix of light- and heavyweight fabrics used side-by-side can put a strain on the work and may result in poor wear.

You will be starting from scratch for some projects, in which case you are likely to buy all the fabrics that you need in one go. When it comes to designing your own projects, however, having a good 'stash' of fabrics can be a great starting point. Save leftovers from projects, buy fabrics you like as you see them, and keep old scraps of garments (as long as the fabric is clean and in good condition).

Fusible webbing

Double-sided adhesive webbing makes very light work of appliqué (see page 118) and is ideal for quilting beginners. Not only does it allow you to attach cut-out fabric shapes to a backing fabric with ease, but it also prevents the shapes from fraying.

Fusible webbing comes attached to backing paper, which can be used like tracing paper for transferring a design accurately before ironing it to a fabric. It can give a slightly firmer feel to appliqué shapes than the hand-sewn equivalent, but does not tend to be a problem.

Once you have bonded appliqué shapes onto a backing fabric, you can machine-sew around the edges in satin stitch. Make sure you always follow the manufacturer's instructions when using fusible webbing.

Interfacing

Interfacing is a special, non-woven product used for stiffening fabric. It is particularly useful for projects such as bags, where it can be used for firming up the base and handles.

Interfacing comes in different weights and softnesses, and the easiest type to use is the iron-on variety. As long as you follow the manufacturer's instructions carefully when bonding interfacing, items made using it can be washed or cleaned in the usual way.

Thread

The best machine-sewing thread for making quilts is cotton, particularly if working with cotton fabrics. A polyester/cotton blend can also be used and tends to be stronger than pure cotton.

If you are sewing patches together for a multicoloured quilt, it can be difficult to know what colour thread to use. Unless there is a predominant fabric colour, choose a neutral colour such as dark beige or medium grey. If the fabrics tend to be in dark colours, use a dark grey, navy or black. Always make sure the tension is correct in your machine to avoid stitches showing between patches, which can look unsightly if the thread isn't a good match.

For tacking (basting) use a contrast colour. Avoid using dark thread on light fabric however, because it may leave fibres behind on removal, making the fabric look dirty. Be sure to use colourfast thread, too, so that the colour does not transfer to your fabric. Don't be tempted to use cheap thread, either: tacking thread is stronger than normal sewing thread and is less likely to break.

Quilting thread is much stronger than usual sewing thread, and is often wax coated to make it slightly stiffer. This means it is not ideal for machine-quilting as it can stick, but is perfect for quilting by hand.

Invisible quilting thread, which comes in clear and smoke, is good for quilting multicoloured projects because it doesn't show up. It is also known as nylon monofilament thread and invisible nylon thread. Invisible quilting thread may melt if you use a very hot iron on it.

Machine-embroidery thread, which is thicker than standard thread, can be used for quilting if you wish the stitches to be prominent.

Wadding (batting)

Wadding is the soft padding that usually makes up the middle part of the quilt 'sandwich' (see page 111). Even in these days of metrication, wadding still tends to be sold in ounces.

Polyester is the most popular wadding material, and 70g (2oz) is the most suitable weight. Heavier weights are available, but anything thicker than 135g (4oz) can be very difficult to work with. The most usual colour for polyester wadding is white, but it is also available in black for use with dark fabrics so any 'bearding' will not show.

Always buy the best-quality wadding you can afford. Some polyester varieties compact irrevocably when ironed – these tend to have a slightly crispy feel to them. Soft, silky wadding is more resilient and drapes better when an item is finished. Opt for bonded waddings where possible. Here, the fibres are treated with resin or glue to prevent them shifting about inside the quilt once it is made and you are unlikely to have problems with bearding. The resin does not affect the drape or handle of the wadding.

Cotton wadding is the main alternative to polyester. It gives quite a different feel and lends more of an 'antique' look to a project. Cotton-wadded quilts look much flatter, but they are heavier and warmer, which may make them too warm for a child's bed. In the past, cotton-wadded quilts required very close quilting to hold the wadding in place, as it tended to pull apart with use. This is why antique quilts are often very densely quilted. Modern needled-cotton waddings are a great improvement, however. They are more stable and the fibres are less likely to pull apart.

Cotton wadding is more costly than polyester, but comes in very wide widths, which is great for making larger quilts. Cotton wadding is also a good option for wall hangings, where you want the quilt to hang flat. Manufacturers may recommend that you wash cotton wadding carefully before making up a project and you will need to follow such recommendations carefully.

Wadding can be bought from a roll or in pre-cut packs of standard sizes. In some instances the wadding will come with instructions as to how closely a project should be quilted and how to wash it. Sample packs of wadding are available so you can try out different options. Iron-on wadding does not need quilting into place. It is fairly thin and most useful for wadding smaller parts of a project, rather than an entire quilt.

Equipment

Quilting can be carried out with the minimum of equipment and if you sew regularly you will probably have most items already. There are certain tools and gadgets that are popular with quilters, which will allow you to work faster and more accurately. As your

interest in patchwork grows, it is a good idea to look out for specialist patchwork and quilting shops and fairs, where you can pick up the more unusual products.

Basic kit

There are a number of tools that are standard in a quilter's basic equipment.

Pencil

Scissors

Safety pins

Tape measure

Calculator

Ruler

Iron

Thimble

Pins and pincushion
Long pins are best for quilting – at least 2.5cm (1in).

Needles
Machine-sewing: universal needle sizes 70 and 80 are suitable for quilting. Hand-sewing: short needles, called 'betweens' are used for hand-quilting.

Sewing machine
At the most basic level, you can use a machine that does just straight stitches, while a swing-needle machine, which does zigzag stitches, is useful for projects requiring appliqué work. There are some dedicated quilting machines on the market, as well as some that are capable of a wide range of embroidery stitches.

Erasable fabric marker pens
Erasable markers make easy work of transferring designs and motifs onto fabric (see page 119). There are two types: vanishing and water-soluble.

With either type of erasable marker, it is very important not to iron over the marks before attempting to remove them: this can set them and render them permanent. Having erased water-soluble marker lines, it is also important to allow the fabric to dry completely before pressing or ironing, otherwise the lines may reappear and, again, become difficult or impossible to remove.

Tailor's chalk
The easiest way to use chalk is in the form of a dressmaker's chalk pencil.

Chalk is particularly useful for dark fabrics, which can otherwise be difficult to mark effectively, and you can usually remove it simply by brushing it off or wiping it over with a damp cloth. Chalk lines are not usually clear enough to be used for transferring embroidery motifs to fabric.

Quilting clips

These are round metal clips that are used for keeping a quilt rolled up and out of the way while you are machining a particular part of it (bicycle clips can be used instead).

Optional extras

In addition to your basic kit there are other pieces of equipment that can make life easier and speed up some of the quilt-making processes.

Rotary cutter

This gadget allows you to cut several layers of fabric at once and increases accuracy at the same time. They must always be used with a self-healing cutting mat, pushing the gadget away from you through the fabric, rather than pulling it towards you.

Self-healing cutting mat

These come in two thicknesses. The thinner mats are suitable for use with rotary cutters only, while the thicker ones can also be used with craft knives. Rest on a hard, even surface when cutting and keep flat and away from radiators, heaters and direct sunlight when not in use to prevent distortion and buckling.

Squared paper

A pad of paper with 5mm (3⅛in) faint squares is ideal for planning designs and working out fabric quantities. You can draw your designs to scale, using a number of squares to represent 10cm (4in).

Basting spray

This is an aerosol glue that can be used to hold the layers of a quilt together for stitching without the need for pinning and basting. The glue is simply sprayed onto the wrong side of both the backing fabric and the quilt top and, once the glue is tacky, the surfaces are pressed together. The adhesion lessens over time, and the glue washes out when you launder the quilt. Sometimes it has a strong chemical smell, which really makes it unsuitable for use on quilts for babies.

'O' weights

These circular plastic weights have small spikes in the bottom that grip fabric when you stand them on it. They are very useful for holding fabric flat on the floor or keeping it steady on the table while you cut it.

Tape-maker

This is a metal, funnel-shaped gadget used for converting a strip of fabric into professional-looking binding. They come in different widths and are not adjustable, so you need a different size for each width of binding.

Seam ripper or unpicker

This is an essential tool for quick unpicking of machine stitching. Use the tool with care to avoid tearing the fabric with its sharp point.

Embroidery hoop

This is a metal and plastic or wooden hoop over which you stretch fabric when embroidering it to prevent the fabric puckering.

Seam gauge

This is a small, adjustable gadget for setting a specific measurement – useful for making turnings.

Light box

If you intend to do much sewing a light box would be a very useful acquisition. It is ideal for tracing through light-coloured fabric for embroidery and for reversing a design for appliqué by tracing over the back of a photocopy. You can buy small light boxes quite cheaply. Taping your work to a sunny window works almost as well, but isn't quite so comfortable to work at.

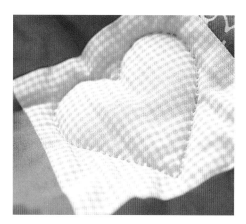

Patchwork & Quilting Techniques

Almost all of the projects share similar patchwork and quilting techniques. Once you have built up a little skill, the steps will start to become second nature to you.

Patchwork

Also known as piecing, patchwork involves stitching small, geometrical patches of patterned fabrics together to form a larger design. Accuracy is vital, since a small discrepancy can result in a big error across the width of a quilt. This means any templates and cutting out must be precise, as must your sewing.

Joining patches

Patches have very narrow seam allowances, which can be fiddly to sew. For greater flexibility and to make the sewing easier a wider allowance of 1cm (⅜in) or 1.5cm (⅝in) is used for most of the projects in this book.

1 Sewing accurately along the seam lines is very important, so mark them on the back of each shape using a second, smaller template. Centre the smaller template on the back of each fabric shape and draw around it.

2 Lay the patches out, right side up, in the order you wish them to appear. In many projects, the patches in the horizontal rows are joined first and then the rows are joined from top to bottom to form the quilt panel.

3 When you come to join the rows together, mark the row number in the seam allowance of each left-most square. This way you will also know which is the left-hand end of each row.

4 Pin the shapes together in the correct order, right sides together. You can check that the seams line up with each other by pushing a pin through before you attach each square to its neighbour (✂ 4).

5 Machine-sew along all the seams, with the pins on the top surface of the fabric and the bulk of the fabric to your left. The pins should have their heads towards you for easy removal (✂ 5). Sew along the marked seam lines and take the pins out as you sew. Don't sew over pins as this can break the needle. Press all the seams open.

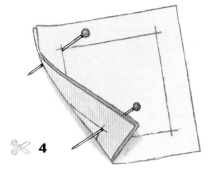

✂ **4**

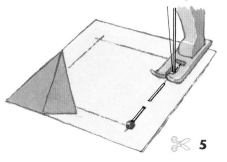

✂ **5**

Chaining

Also known as chain piecing, or the flag method, chaining is a quick way to machine-stitch several patches in one go. Pin the patches together, inserting the pins along the seam line with the heads towards you for easy removal. Feed the patches under the presser foot one after the other, with a short gap between each. Don't stop or cut the thread. You will end up with a string of patches connected together. Snip them apart and press.

Joining rows

Lay out the rows, right side up, one above the other. Pin each row to the next along the seam line, right sides facing. Ensure you match up the seams in each row. Machine-sew the strips together (see below) and press all seams open.

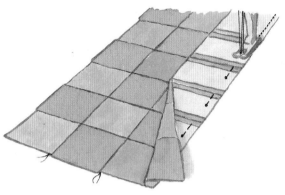

The quilt 'sandwich'

A quilt consists of a top, the wadding (batting) and the backing. Together they are known as the quilt 'sandwich'.

The backing fabric

Patchwork projects often have pieced fronts, but when the back doesn't show, such as on bedding, a wall hanging or a cushion cover, it is cut simply from one piece of fabric. Try to choose a backing fabric that coordinates with the patchwork front and is of a similar weight.

For larger quilts standard-width quilting fabric isn't sufficiently wide for the backing. You have two choices: the first is to buy wider-width fabric such as cotton sheeting; the second is to join lengths of standard-width fabric. The simplest way is to buy double the length of fabric that you need and join it so you have one seam down the centre of the quilt back. Trim equal amounts from either side of the joined fabric to reduce it to the required width.

Another way is to buy two lengths of fabric the size of the quilt. Position one length in the centre and cut strips from the other length to join to either side of the central panel. Remember to add an extra 3cm (1¼in) to the width for seam allowances when calculating the width of the side strips. A third way to join widths of fabric for a backing is to use the fabric sideways.

Assembling the layers

Follow these instructions for a conventional quilt with bound edges. (For a 'bagged-out' quilt, see page 120).

1 Press the quilt top and backing fabric and trim the backing to the correct size if necessary, following the instructions for the project.

2 If the wadding is creased, lay it flat for a day then cut it to the correct size. You may have to join two strips of wadding if you can't buy a piece wide enough. To join wadding, butt the long edges together but don't overlap them. Using white sewing thread and a large herringbone or oversewing stitch (see page 117), sew the two pieces together through the front of the wadding. Don't pull the stitches too tight or you will get a bump in the quilt. Turn the wadding over and repeat on the back to ensure a strong join.

3 To make the quilt 'sandwich', lay the backing fabric on the floor, wrong side up if it has right and wrong sides. Smooth the fabric out completely flat without stretching it – 'O' weights are helpful here (see page 109) – or you can hold the fabric to the floor with strips of masking tape. Lay the wadding on the backing, ensuring the edges align. Smooth out any wrinkles, but don't stretch the wadding.

4 Place the quilt top on the wadding, right side up. Smooth it out, checking that any joins or seam lines that are supposed to be straight really are straight. If your wadding is larger than the quilt top, ensure there is an even border extending all round the edge.

5 The three layers of the quilt have to be held together so they cannot shift about while they are being quilted. The easiest way to do this is to pin-baste the quilt.

Pin-basting

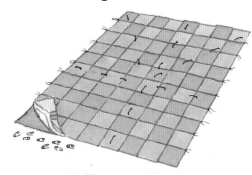

The conventional way to hold the layers together is to tack them, but the quickest way – which is also very effective – is to pin the layers together with safety pins. This is known as 'pin-basting' (see above).

You will need a very generous number of safety pins. Curved quilting pins are easiest to use. (It is much quicker to insert the pins if you open a batch of them first, rather than opening each one as you use it.)

Pin the quilt from the outside edges towards the centre. The pins should be no more than about 10cm (4in) apart. Do not pin very close to any seams or any lines that you will be quilting along. Make sure you keep the layers as flat as possible and do not distort or pucker them as you pin. You will need to reach under the quilt with one hand to guide the pins, so, again, try to keep the quilt as flat as possible when you do this.

Machine-quilting

You need to sew through all the layers to prevent them from shifting. For speed, machine-quilting is the best option, although hand-quilting has a quality that is more appropriate for some projects. Some sewing machines can do a convincing mock hand-quilting stitch. However, for most of the projects in this book a standard straight machine-stitch is most appropriate.

Use a slightly longer stitch than for normal sewing, and always check the tension of your machine on scraps of fabric first. Make up a miniature quilt by putting an offcut of wadding between two pieces of the sort of fabric you have used for the quilt top and backing and sew along it a few times. Check for any puckering.

On some occasions you will be marking lines on the quilt top and stitching along them; on others you will be quilting along the seams joining the patchwork shapes. This is known as 'stitching-in-the-ditch'.

Stitching-in-the-ditch

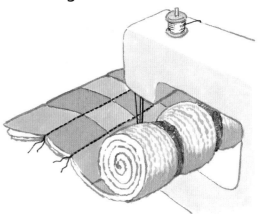

Use invisible quilting thread in the top of your machine and cotton sewing thread in the bobbin in a colour to match the back of the quilt. Sew along the seams between the patchwork pieces that make up the quilt top. As you sew, follow the seams exactly, parting them with your hands to allow the stitches to sink into the seam. This is why this type of quilting is known as 'stitching-in-the-ditch'.

Always stitch the vertical seams first. To avoid the quilt puckering, sew in one direction only, starting from the same end or side of the quilt and working across towards the other. You will find that you have to feed a bulk of quilt through your sewing machine when you sew the left-hand seams.

To make this material easier to handle, roll the quilt up fairly tightly, so the seam you are about to sew is exposed just to the left of the roll. Prevent the roll from coming loose by holding it in place with quilting clips (see page 109).

Hand-quilting

Although much slower than machine-quilting, hand-quilting has the advantage that you can sit and do it in an armchair in the evening while watching television and you can pick it up and put it down according to your mood.

The stitch used for quilting is a small running stitch. You will need a 'betweens' needle and some hand-quilting thread (see pages 107 and 108). If you are short of time you can use fairly large stitches, up to 1cm (⅜in) long, although smaller stitches will always look neater. When hand-quilting, the needle should pass vertically up and down through the fabric, with your sewing hand always above the fabric and your other hand always below it to receive the needle and pass it back.

You will need to wear a thimble, at least on your sewing hand. Special quilter's thimbles are also available to protect the fingers of the lower hand, as you have to receive the needle by feeling for it, and this can make your fingers sore.

Tying a quilt

Tying is a very quick alternative to conventional quilting, and can be used to hold the three layers of a quilt together. Its effects are best with higher loft waddings, and it is the easiest technique to use with thicker fillings.

1 Plan out the positions for the ties. If you have used good-quality bonded wadding, the ties do not have to be very close together. Approximately 20cm (8in) is fine. Mark the tie positions on the quilt top using tailor's chalk or vanishing marker to make small dots.

2 For speed, you can make all the ties in each horizontal row in one go, although this means they must all be the same colour. Begin with the top row of dots on the right-hand side of the quilt (on the left if you are left-handed). Take one piece of soft embroidery thread, stranded cotton or sewing ribbon. This should be as long as the quilt is wide. Don't knot it. Thread it through a crewel (embroidery) needle and take a small stitch through the dot, straight down through all thicknesses of the quilt, leaving an end of 10cm (4in). Bring the needle back up to the right side, to the left (right, if you are left-handed) of the point where the needle went into the fabric. Without cutting

the thread, make the same sort of stitch through the next dot. Pull the thread just tight enough between the dots so that it lies flat on the surface of the quilt. Continue until you have completed the whole line. Repeat with another length of thread, sewing through the same holes, or as close as possible to them. You now have two threads passing through the row.

3 Repeat this process with each row, always working from right to left.

4 Cut the threads between the stitches and tie the ends into reef knots. Trim the ends to between 2.5–7.5cm (1–3in) depending on the age of the child. The younger the child, the shorter the end should be.

Buttoning

For older children, where the risk of choking is not an issue, buttons can be a fun and interesting alternative to tying a quilt. Choose small buttons in colours and designs that coordinate with the fabrics.

1 Plan the positions of the buttons and mark dots as for tying (see above).

2 Sew a small button on each dot, ensuring you stitch it on firmly and knot off the ends securely on the wrong side of the quilt.

Embroidery & Appliqué Techniques

In this section you will find instructions for the embroidery stitches used in the projects, tips on machine-embroidery and basic appliqué techniques.

If you don't have time to embroider details on a project, you can, in most cases, draw the design onto the fabric using indelible markers. Always test a pen first on a scrap of the same fabric to check its effect, then heat-set following the manufacturer's instructions and wash the sample piece for colourfastness before working on the item itself.

Hand-embroidery

When choosing fabric to embroider on, make sure that it is reasonably firm and that any embroidery cotton running across the back of the fabric will not be visible from the front. Thin fabrics are not recommended.

You will need stranded embroidery thread for the projects in this book. This thread is sold in skeins, where six separate strands of thread are twisted together. The strands have to be separated into groups of two or three for embroidery. Cut off a length of thread about 40cm (16in) and then separate it carefully into two lots of three strands, or three lots of two strands.

Use an embroidery frame for your work, choosing one that is a suitable size for the project, but not so large that it is awkward to hold.

1 Mark your design onto the fabric following the instructions on page 119.

2 Stretch the fabric over the frame. Don't worry if the motif is too large to fit into the frame. You can move the fabric around on the frame as you complete parts of the embroidery.

3 Thread a crewel needle with a piece of thread about 40cm (16in) long.

Don't knot the end of the thread. Insert the threaded needle into your work on the wrong side of the fabric and pull the thread up through it, leaving a loose end of about 4cm (1½in). Make a couple of tiny backstitches to lock the thread in place.

4 Work the embroidery (see below for specific stitches).

5 When you have just a small length of thread left, take the needle through to the wrong side of your work and pass the needle down through the back of the last few stitches you have worked. Trim off the remainder.

6 To complete the piece, thread the needle with the loose end you left at the start of the work, pass it through the back of the first stitches you made and trim off the remainder.

Embroidery stitches

Different embroidery stitches have different qualities and are suitable for different effects. Here we give instructions for how to work the stitches referred to in the projects.

Running stitch

This is the simplest stitch to carry out, resulting in a broken line of short, even stitches with an equal amount of space between them. It is worked from right to left, unless you are left-handed. Start at the right end of the sewing line, and work in a constant forward direction. Several stitches can be picked up on the needle before it is pulled through.

Backstitch

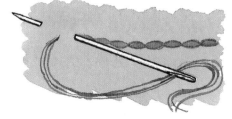

A useful, easy and versatile stitch for sewing an accurate solid line. The smaller the stitches, the more precisely the line will follow curved and irregular shapes. Begin at the right-hand end of a line (or the left-hand end if you are left-handed), and bring the needle up to the right side of the fabric one stitch length from

the end of that line. Make a small backstitch by putting the needle back into the fabric at the end of the line. Now bring the needle up to the right side of the fabric once again, this time a stitch length beyond the point where the needle first came up (see left). This stitch will be twice as long as the first. Take the needle back to the wrong side of the fabric through the first point and continue in this way.

Cross-stitch

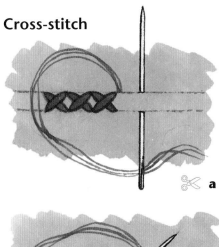

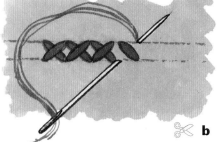

Working between two guidelines, bring the needle up at the left-hand end of the top line and take it back down at the right-hand end of the

bottom line, forming a diagonal stitch at 45 degrees to the guidelines. Bring the needle up in the right-hand end of the top line (✂ a) and take it down again at the left-hand end of the bottom line, immediately below the point where the needle first emerged. You should have a diagonal cross that will fit neatly into a square. You are now in the correct position to make another stitch. Continue in this way, being sure to keep each stitch neat and 'square' (✂ b).

Chainstitch

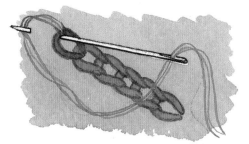

This linked stitch, which looks like a fine chain, is useful for making decorative lines. Bring the needle to the right side of the fabric at the beginning of a line. Pull the thread through and hold it with your other thumb so that a loop is created when you insert the needle back at the same point. Now bring the needle to the right side again, within the loop, but a stitch length along the line. Pull it through the loop, but do not pull too tight (see above).

Satin stitch

This is the best stitch to use for creating a flat area of colour. You need to work between a pair of guidelines, or a marked-out solid shape. The stitches can be straight or diagonal but must always be close together and parallel, and look smooth, neat and flat. Bring the needle to the right side at a point on the left-hand guide of the space to be filled. Take the thread across the design, and insert the needle through a point on the guide on the right-hand side. Carry the needle across the back of the work and bring it out again just below the point where you first started (see above).

Pressing embroidery
Place the work face down on an ironing board and smooth it out flat. Lay a damp cloth over the back of the work and press with a hot, dry iron, lifting the iron up and down in a deliberate pressing motion, rather than pushing the iron along as you do when ironing clothes.

Stem stitch

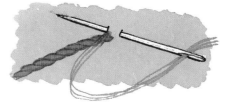

This stitch creates a wider line than backstitch, but is used similarly to create a solid line. It is sometimes known as outline or crewel stitch. Work from left to right, unless you are left-handed. Bring the needle to the right side of the fabric at the left-hand end of the line you are embroidering, and slightly above the line. Insert the needle a little way along the line to the right, and slightly below the line. This creates a small stitch that crosses the line at an angle. Pull the thread through and make another stitch at the same angle, close to the first one so the stitches slightly overlap. Continue in this way ensuring the stitches are even and parallel to their neighbours (see above).

Machine-embroidery

Some sewing machines have a variety of embroidery stitches. These can be very useful for crazy patchwork (see page 90), where you need to embroider along the seams where the patches join. You will need to use machine-embroidery thread for this.

Follow the sewing-machine manufacturer's instructions carefully for setting up the embroidery programme (the setting of the tension and stitch length are vitally important) and always test the stitch out on a scrap piece of fabric first to check for puckering and to ensure the stitch is well formed.

Machine-embroidery has been recommended for the crazy patchwork project in this book (see page 90), but if your machine cannot do these stitches, you can work the seam lines by hand instead. Below are the traditional hand-stitches used for crazy patchwork. You will need to use three strands of stranded embroidery thread in colours that contrast well with your patchwork fabrics.

Chevron stitch

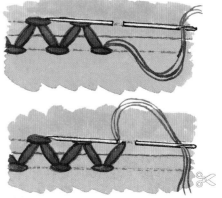

This stitch is worked from left to right. Start by drawing two parallel guidelines on either side of the patchwork seam and follow ✂ a to create a zigzag effect between the two lines.

Herringbone stitch

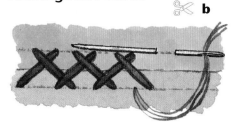

Start by drawing two parallel guidelines on either side of the patchwork seam and work from left to right (reverse the instructions if you are left-handed) to complete the stitch following ✂ b.

Feather stitch

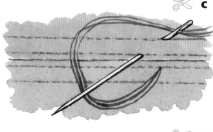

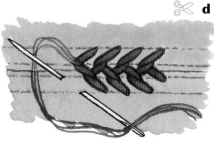

Start by drawing four equally spaced parallel guidelines with the patchwork seam running between the centre two lines (✂ c). Follow ✂ d to complete the stitch.

Hand-sewing stitches

Even if you are using a machine to make a project, you will still need to do a little hand-sewing, usually to finish off your work. Hand-stitches are usually worked from right to left, unless you are left-handed, in which case you need to reverse the instructions and work from left to right.

Tacking (basting)

This is temporary stitching, usually in a contrasting colour, which is used to hold fabric in place while it is being machined. Knot the thread at the end, and make simple running stitches about 6–10mm (¼–⅜in) long and the same distance apart. Sometimes it is useful to tack along the seam line so that you can use this as a guideline when you machine. However, this can make removing the tacking tricky, so you may wish to tack close to, but not exactly on the seam line.

Herringbone stitch

This stitch is used to join wadding (batting) together (see page 111). Use a suitable colour sewing thread. Knot the end of the thread, insert the needle into the wadding and give a short, sharp tug. This should embed the knot in the wadding. Then follow the instructions given for herringbone as an embroidery stitch.

Oversewing

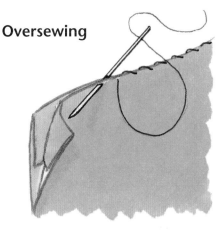

This is a useful, general-purpose hand-stitch that is used to seal two or more layers of fabric – openings after turning right sides out, for example – or for finishing off the corners of binding. It is worked from right to left, unless you are left-handed. Hold the work flat, with the edges to be sewn pointing away from you. Knot the thread and, working from the right-hand end of the seam, pass the needle between the two layers to be sewn and bring it out to the front of the layer of fabric closest to you, close to the top of the fold. You will pick up just a few threads of the fabric. Pull the needle through, take it round to the back of the work and insert it close to the fold, a little way along from where the needle first came out. Bring the needle straight towards you, through the top of both folds, again picking up just a few threads. Continue in this way, making a row of tiny neat stitches that are quite close together (see above).

Slip-hemming

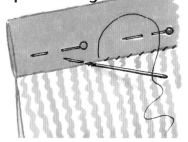

This stitch is useful for attaching binding to the back of a quilt. Work from right to left unless you are left-handed, in which case you should work from left to right. Knot the thread, insert the needle under the right-hand end of the binding and bring the needle to the front, close to the edge of the binding. Pick up a couple of threads from the backing fabric, just below and a small way to the left of the point where the needle first emerged. Before pulling the needle through, also pick up a couple of threads from the edge of the binding. Pull the thread through and continue in this way, spacing the stitches equally. This stitch will not show on the right side of the quilt because you sew only through the back of the binding and the backing fabric (see above).

Appliqué

The easiest, quickest and, possibly, neatest way to carry out appliqué is to use fusible webbing. Be sure to use your webbing economically by working along the edges first and placing your motifs fairly close together. If you follow the manufacturer's instructions carefully, you should be able to launder the finished item with no problems. Sewing around the edge of the shapes in satin stitch will increase their durability.

1 Turn the webbing so that the paper side is uppermost. Reverse your motif (you will be working on the back of the fabric) and trace it onto the paper with a sharp pencil. Cut out the motif, leaving a small margin of paper around the edge of the shape.

2 Lay your appliqué fabric wrong side up on an ironing board. Place your cut-out motif fibre-side down onto the fabric. Iron the motif in place, holding for 3 to 4 seconds with dry heat, to transfer the adhesive web onto the back of the fabric.

3 Using a small pair of sharp fabric scissors, cut out the motif carefully along the pencil lines.

4 Peel off the paper backing. Lay the motif in the correct position on the backing fabric, adhesive side down. Cover with a damp cloth and press lightly for about 8 to 10 seconds. Lift the iron and press each part of the motif, picking up the iron and putting it down deliberately each time you move it.

Using satin stitch on appliqué

Once you have bonded the appliqué motif onto the backing fabric, you may wish to neaten the edges with stitching. On traditional appliqué this is usually done by hand, but most sewing machines do a good zigzag or satin stitch, and with a little practice you can achieve very professional-looking results. Machine-stitching is stronger than hand-stitching and, once machined around, appliqué shapes are more hard-wearing and less difficult to launder.

Set the sewing machine to a close zigzag satin stitch, about half the maximum width. (Refer to your sewing-machine manual and experiment with different stitch lengths and widths on scrap fabric before starting on the actual project.)

Sew carefully around the motif, keeping the edge of the shape in the very centre of the presser foot at all times. Work fairly slowly at a constant speed. To work a corner, sew right into it and, leaving the needle in the fabric, lift the presser foot to turn the fabric in a new direction. Lower the presser foot and continue sewing.

Once you have completed the sewing, leave a long end of thread. Pull this through to the back of the fabric and knot the ends of both threads or pass them through a needle and run them through the back of your stitching to finish off.

Transferring Designs

For a number of projects in this book you will be working with templates, which often need to be enlarged and then transferred to fabric.

Enlarging designs

The simplest method for enlarging templates, patterns and designs is to use a photocopier that has an enlarging facility. If a design has been reduced by fifty per cent (half size) you will have to enlarge it by two hundred per cent (double the size) to get it to the correct measurement.

Squaring up

If you don't have access to a photocopier, you can enlarge a design by squaring up. This is a simple and reliable method that has been used by artists and designers for centuries. Draw a grid of 1.25cm (½in) squares over the motif to be enlarged, and plot a larger grid on a plain sheet of paper. The squares of the larger grid must be enlarged by the same amount you wish to enlarge the motif. For example, if you want the motif four times bigger, your larger squares need to be 5cm (2in) square. Transfer freehand what you see in each small

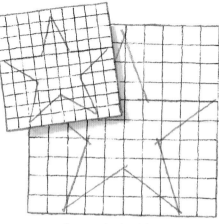

square to the equivalent larger square. So, if a line crosses a square in the middle on the small grid, you know to draw the line in the middle of the corresponding square on the bigger grid (see above).

Transferring markings

Once you have your patterns or motifs enlarged to the correct size, there are a number of methods you can use to transfer them to the fabric for cutting out, embroidering or quilting. See page 108 for details of suitable markers and pencils to use for transferring designs.

1 To cut out shapes for patchwork or appliqué, use your pattern to make a template then draw the design on the back of your fabric in pencil so that any cutting lines are concealed. Bear in mind that when working on the back of fabric, asymmetrical motifs need to be reversed.

2 To embroider simple designs (such as heart shapes) you can transfer the design to the fabric by drawing round a template on the front of the fabric using a vanishing marker.

3 More complex embroidery designs need more detail and the easiest way to transfer them is to use a light box. First trace or photocopy the design onto thin paper (such as tracing paper, typing paper or layout paper). Place the tracing on the light box, switch it on, then lay the pressed fabric over the top, right side up (if applicable). Ensure the motif is in the correct position, then trace it using a vanishing fabric marker or a pencil.

Finishing & Binding

The final stage of making a quilt is to bind it or to finish the edges in some other way, and there are several ways of doing this.

'Bagging out'

This is probably the simplest way to finish a quilt because it avoids having to bind the edges at all.

1 Lay out the backing fabric, right side up. Spread the top fabric on it, wrong side up. The right sides of both fabrics will be facing each other. Check all the edges of the fabrics are neatly aligned.

2 Machine-stitch the front and back fabric sections together, taking a 1.5cm (⅝in) seam all round and leaving a 50cm (20in) gap at the centre of one of the short ends.

3 Trim the seam allowance to within a few millimetres of the stitching at each corner, cutting across the corner first, then making two further cuts (see Checkers Sleepover Quilt, step 12, page 33). Be very careful not to cut right up to the stitching or to cut the stitching itself.

4 Turn the resulting bag right sides out and poke the corners into shape very carefully and gently using the closed point of a pair of scissors.

5 Press all round the seam edges of the outside of the bag with a steam iron, or with a dry iron and a damp cloth. To get perfect edges, you may need to manipulate them with your fingers as you iron.

6 Use the bag as a template to cut out a rectangle of wadding exactly the same size. Be very careful not to cut the edges of the bag as you do this.

7 Insert the wadding into the bag, pushing the corners of the wadding well into the corners. Hold the wadding in place at the corners of the bag on the outside with bulldog clips, strong clothes pegs or large safety pins. Shake the quilt gently and smooth it out to ensure the wadding is evenly distributed.

8 Oversew the opening then pin-baste the quilt following the instructions on page 112. Complete the quilt according to the project steps.

Binding a quilt

The most common way to finish a quilt is to neaten the raw edges by sewing binding, or long thin fabric strips, around them. These strips can be cut either from the straight grain of a fabric, or on the bias. You need sufficient strips to go all round the edge of the quilt, allowing a little extra for turnings. Where straight binding is used for a project, dimensions are given. If you need to make bias binding, follow the instructions below.

Making bias binding

1 Place your fabric in front of you widthways, right side up. Fold up the bottom left-hand corner at 45 degrees, so that the left-hand edge lines up with the top edge of the fabric. Iron a crease, open the fabric out flat and cut along the fold (✂ 1).

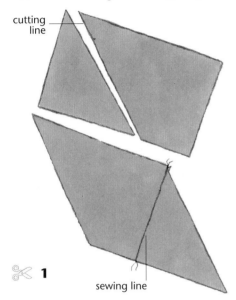

cutting line

sewing line

✂ **1**

2 Keeping the triangle of fabric the same way up with right side uppermost, place it to the right of the larger piece so the short edges abut. Keeping the short edges touching, flip the triangle to the left onto the larger piece of fabric. The short edges should still align and the right sides of the fabric are now facing.

3 Pin, then machine-stitch, along the short edge and press the seam open.

4 Draw parallel lines on the fabric, aligning with the left-hand diagonal, and cut along the lines to form a series of strips (✂ 4).

✂ **4**

5 Join the strips to each other by aligning the diagonal ends and machine-stitching parallel to the end (✂ 5). If you are joining several strips at once, check that your seams are all on the correct side of the fabric. Press the seams open, being careful not to stretch the strips as you press them. Trim off the corners of the seams that project beyond the edge of the binding.

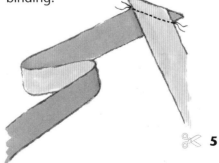

✂ **5**

Preparing the binding strips

Whether the binding is made from straight or bias strips, once you have cut them (and, if necessary, joined them) you will need to press them before sewing them onto the quilt.

1 First press each strip in half lengthways, wrong sides facing. Open out the fold and press a 1.5cm (⅝in) or 1cm (⅜in) turning along one long edge (this will be equivalent to the seam allowance for the project) and a 1cm (⅜in) turning along the other (✂ 1). If you wish to hand-finish the binding (see below), press a 1.5cm (⅝in) turning along both edges if this is the seam allowance for the project.

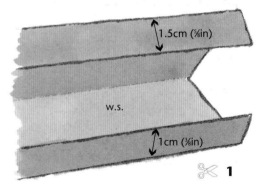

1.5cm (⅝in)

w.s.

1cm (⅜in)

✂ **1**

2 Open out the first turning and press it again lightly so you can still see the crease but the fabric is opened out flat.

Attaching the binding

Each project will specify whether to start with the long or short sides of the quilt. For this example, we start with the long sides.

1 Lay the quilt sandwich out flat on the floor with the top surface uppermost. Pin the two shorter binding strips to the long ends of the quilt top, right sides facing. The 1.5cm (⅝in) pressed seam allowance should be closest to the raw edge of the quilt and equal amounts of binding should project beyond the ends (see ✂ 1). The wadding and backing may project beyond the edges of the quilt, but don't worry about this. Machine-stitch along the pressed fold using matching sewing thread.

2 Press the binding away from the centre of the quilt (do not press the seam open), then take the binding to the wrong side, folding along the centre line. If the wadding and backing project too far, trim them neatly, parallel to the edge of the quilt top, just enough to allow you to fold the binding over it along the centre fold. Press the binding along the centre fold and re-press the 1cm (⅜in) turning so the raw edge is still folded under.

3 Pin the binding to the back of the quilt so that the folded edge extends over the machine-stitching you have just done by about 3 or 4mm (⅛in) (see ✂ 3). Pin the binding in place on the back of the quilt, then transfer the pins one by one to the front of the quilt, so they lie along the binding seam.

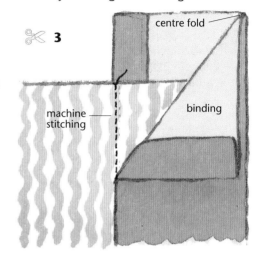

✂ **3**

4 Using invisible thread in the top of your machine and thread to match the backing fabric in the bobbin, stitch-in-the-ditch along the pinned binding seams (see page 112). This will catch the binding in place on the back of the quilt. Trim the ends of the binding level with the long sides of the quilt.

5 Repeat the above steps with the two remaining binding strips on the short edges of the quilt. But before pressing the binding to the wrong side along the centre fold, trim the ends of the binding so they extend 2.5cm (1in) beyond the edges of the quilt on either side. Fold these ends to the wrong side, so the fold is level with the long edges of the quilt, and press.

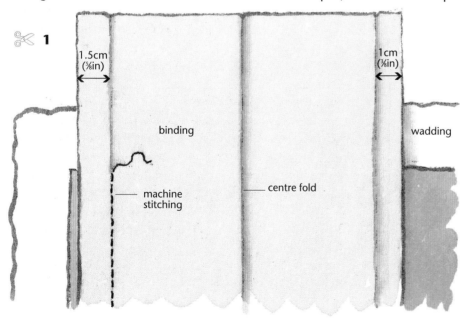

✂ **1**

Now fold the binding to the wrong side along the centre fold and press (see ✂ 5). Pin the binding in place along the seam line as before.

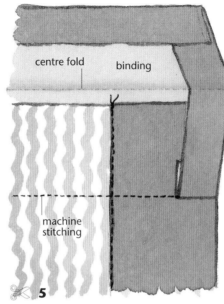

centre fold   binding

machine stitching

✂ 5

6 Stitch-in-the-ditch along the pinned binding seams and oversew the openings at the corners of the binding to neaten (see page 117).

Alternatives

Once step 3 is complete, you can pin the binding along the sewing line on the back of the quilt and hand-stitch it in place using slip-hemming (see page 118).

The all-in-one method

Used for the Alphabet Quilt on page 74, this quick method results in a quilt that looks as though the edges have been separately bound, but in fact they are made from the backing fabric. The backing needs to be about 8cm (3⅛in) larger all round than the quilt top, depending on the width of 'binding' you require.

1 Once you have made the quilt top, spread the wadding out on the floor and centre the quilt top on it. Cut the wadding 1.5cm (⅝in) larger all round than the quilt top.

2 Lay the backing fabric out on the floor wrong side up, if applicable. Centre the quilt top and the wadding on the backing fabric. Cut the fabric 8cm (3⅛in) larger all round than the wadding.

3 Pin-baste the whole quilt and, using invisible thread in the top of your machine and cotton thread to match the backing fabric in the bobbin, quilt along all seam lines by stitching-in-the-ditch (see page 112).

4 Starting at the long sides, fold the extended part of the backing fabric in half along its length, then fold onto the front of the quilt and pin to form a 4cm (1½in) binding. Machine the binding in place on the front of the quilt using matching cotton and sewing 5mm (³⁄₁₆in) from the edge of the border.

5 Repeat on the short ends and oversew the corners with matching thread (see page 117).

Converting a Quilt into a Wall Hanging

An outgrown quilt will make an excellent wall hanging. Or perhaps you wish to make a quilt as a wall hanging from the outset. Here are four methods for hanging a quilt on a wall.

Using curtain hooks

A quick way to hang a small quilt is to use a row of clip-on curtain hooks along the top of the quilt. The clips have sharp teeth that can damage the fibres of a quilt, however, so cut some small pieces of fabric to place over the edge of the quilt where you attach a clip. Use plenty of clips and space them evenly to support the weight of the quilt across its width.

Attaching a sleeve

A more permanent solution, and one that is more suited to larger quilts, is to make a hanging sleeve and attach it to the back of a quilt. The most secure method is to add the sleeve when you attach the binding, but it can also be

added once a quilt is complete. For a smaller quilt, such as a cot quilt, one sleeve across the whole width of the quilt is adequate, while a larger quilt will need the sleeve attached in two or three sections with small gaps between.

Attaching a sleeve before binding a quilt

1 Cut a piece of fabric 25cm (10in) deep by the width of the quilt. If you can, use fabric that matches the quilt backing. If your quilt is larger than a cot quilt, divide the strip into two or three equal pieces, and follow the instructions below for each section.

2 Turn the short ends under by 1cm (⅜in), press, then turn under by the same amount again and machine-sew in place.

3 Fold the fabric strip in half lengthways with wrong sides together. Press flat and centre the sleeve along the top edge of the back of the quilt with the raw edges of the strip level with the raw edges of the top of the quilt. Pin the sleeve in place. If you have more than one sleeve, space them out evenly with a gap of approximately 2cm (¾in) between each piece. (If the quilt top is set lower than the top of the wadding and backing fabric, you must move the sleeve down by the same distance that the raw edge of the binding will be from the top edge of the backing when you apply it.) Tack all round the edge of the sleeve.

4 Pin the binding in place on the front of the quilt, following the specific instructions for that project, and machine-stitch the binding along the seam line. This will fasten the tacked sleeve in place at the same time.

5 Follow the project instructions for completing the binding.

6 Press the sleeve flat so that the top fold lies slightly below the top edge of the binding. Oversew the sleeve to the binding along the top edge, ensuring that the stitches are not visible on the front of the quilt.

7 Roll the bottom edge of the sleeve up slightly and evenly along its length, so the sleeve bulges slightly like a small tunnel. Press the bottom edge of the sleeve to form a sharp crease and oversew that in place (✂ 7).

✂ **7**

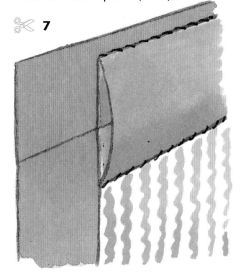

8 Insert the dowel, cut to the same width as the quilt, into the sleeve. It should project beyond the end of the sleeve by 2cm (¾in) at each end. Fix two hooks into the wall at a suitable height and at the right distance to hold the exposed ends of the dowel. Use suitable fixings. If you have more than one sleeve you will need more hooks – positioned where the dowel is exposed. Hang the quilt on the wall by dropping the dowel onto the hooks at both ends.

Attaching a sleeve after binding a quilt

If you decide to convert a quilt into a wall hanging at a later stage, you will need to attach the sleeve(s) by hand, also using a piece of thick dowelling the same width as the quilt.

1 Cut the fabric as above.

2 Fold each strip in half lengthways with wrong sides together. Machine-stitch the long sides together to form a tube (✂ 2a). Turn the raw short ends under by 2cm (¾in) at each end as above (✂ 2b).

3 Pin the sleeve(s) to the back of the quilt, just below the top edge. It should bulge slightly along the length. Oversew the sleeves in place, ensuring that the stitches do not go right through to the front of the quilt. Hang the quilt as above.

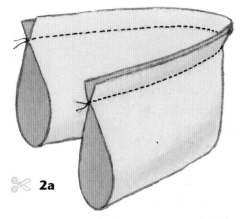

✂ **2a**

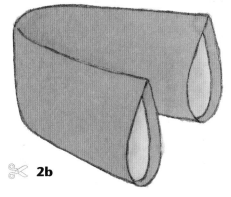

✂ **2b**

Using touch-and-close fastening

This method uses a batten on the wall, rather than hooks and a rod. The quilt is supported evenly along its length and is easy to take down for cleaning. Measure the width of the quilt. You will need a length of 5cm (2in) wide touch-and-close fastening slightly shorter than this measurement. Unless you buy self-adhesive touch-and-close fastening, you will also need a staple gun. Buy a softwood batten the length of the touch-and-close fastening by approximately 7cm (3in) high. Sand and seal the batten before use.

1 Cut a strip of fabric the width of the quilt by approximately 10cm (4in) deep. Turn under all the edges with a 1cm (⅜in) hem and machine-sew in place.

2 Centre the smooth side of the touch-and-close fastening on the right side of the fabric strip and machine-stitch in place close to the long edges of the fastening.

3 Pin this fabric strip close to the top edge of the back of the quilt and oversew or slip-hem in place all round the edge.

4 Centre the other side of the touch-and-close fastening onto the batten. If the fastening is self-adhesive, fix in place following the manufacturer's instructions. If it isn't, staple it to the batten using a staple gun close to the top and bottom edges of the fastening.

5 Fix the batten to the wall in a suitable position, using appropriate fixings. Press the touch-and-close fastening on the back of the quilt onto the strip on the batten.

Hanging with loops

This technique is used for the Safari Wall Pockets on page 54. You will need one loop for every 20cm (8in) of width, plus one extra loop. You will also need a curtain pole slightly wider than the quilt, and a means of attaching it securely to the wall.

1 For each loop, cut a strip of fabric 35cm (13¾in) long by 15cm (6in) wide. As the fabric will be visible on the right side, chose one to match the binding of the quilt, or to coordinate with it.

2 Fold the strips in half lengthways with raw edges level. Pin along the raw edge and sew to form tubes. Press the seams open, turn right sides out and press with the seam in the centre.

3 Fold each strip in half widthways with the seam on the inside and the raw ends level. Turn the raw ends under 1.5cm (⅝in), press then machine-stitch to hold in place. Space the loops equally along the top edge of the back of the quilt with the turnings towards the inside. Make sure they are level at the top to take the weight evenly on the pole. Pin, then oversew, each strip in place.

4 Thread the loops onto the pole and fix it to the wall.

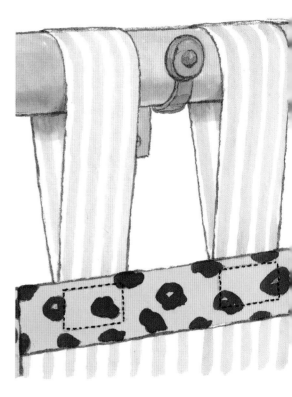

Caring for Quilts

If a quilt is being used on a cot or a child's bed, chances are that it will need laundering. Dry cleaning is never recommended as it can leave dangerous fumes in the fibres, which can be fatal if inhaled by a sleeping child. There are other methods available to you, however.

Washing and cleaning

Quilts in daily use are likely to get dirty and need washing, so you should always pre-wash fabrics before starting a project. If you also use washable wadding, and the quilt has been well made, using good-quality materials, it should be possible to wash it in the normal way.

You may be able to machine-wash a smaller quilt on a gentle, cool cycle with a short spin. You should also be able to dry a small quilt in a tumble drier on a low heat. If you put a large, dry, colourfast towel in with the quilt it will absorb some of the moisture and prevent the quilt from becoming knotted up.

Remove the quilt from the dryer before it has fully dried and lay it out flat to finishing drying. This will help prevent creasing.

If the quilt is too big to go in a machine, you can wash it by hand in a bath. Use a small amount of gentle washing liquid – suitable for hand-washing delicate items. Rinse the quilt several times. Gently squeeze it to remove as much water as possible, but don't wring it or twist it. The quilt will be heavy, so move it out of the bath carefully to prevent damage to the stitching. Place the quilt on colourfast towels and gently try to squeeze out more water. Dry the quilt flat.

Wall hangings

On a quilt being used as a wall hanging there is likely to be build-up of dust, which can rot fabrics. An occasional light going-over with a soft brush and a vacuum on a low suction setting can help offset deterioration. Sunlight will also make fabrics fade and rot over time, so position wall-hung quilts out of direct sunlight.

Storing

If you need to store a quilt, roll it around a large cardboard tube such as are found in the centre of furnishing fabric rolls. Cover the tube first with acid-free tissue paper and wrap the whole thing in a clean sheet. The use of acid-free tissue paper is most important for antique quilts.

If you don't have the room to store a rolled quilt you can fold it. Place a layer of acid-free tissue paper over the quilt first, fold it as large as you have room for, and place it in a pillowcase or cloth bag. Don't store quilts in plastic storage bags as condensation could cause damage. Refold the quilt every few months, making sure you move the fold lines each time.

Making Cushion Covers

Cushions make good projects for beginners as they require only a relatively small area of patchwork for the front and can have a plain back.

For making a square cushion cover with a zipped back, you will need:
- a suitably sized square cushion pad
- a quilted panel for the front of the cushion
- fabric for the backing
- a light-weight zip slightly shorter than the width of the pad
- bias binding (the length should be four times the width of the cushion plus 20cm (8in))
- piping cord (same length as the bias binding)

1 The cushion pad should be the size that you intend the finished cushion to be. Measure the pad and add 3cm (1¼in) to the measurement, then cut a square of fabric this size for the front of the cushion. For a 65cm (25½in) cushion pad, this would mean a 68cm (26¾in) square of fabric.

2 Round off the corners of the cushion front using a saucer as a template.

3 Cut two pieces from the backing fabric each one the same height as the front, by half the width of the front plus 1.5cm (⅝in). For a 65cm (25½in) cushion pad, this would mean two rectangles of fabric 68cm (26¾in) by 35.5cm (14in). Place the two backing pieces on top of each other, right sides together, and round off two corners on one long side as before. Place the two pieces right sides together and stitch along the long, non-rounded side, 6.5cm (2½in) from the top and bottom edges. Tack the rest of the opening shut and press the seams open.

4 Centre the closed zip along the tacked seam of the backing fabric, face down onto the wrong side of the cushion back. Pin in place (✂ 4), then tack the zip along both sides and at either end just beyond the top and bottom stops (the bits that stop the slider going any further).

5 Insert a zipper foot into your machine and adjust it so the needle is to the left of the foot (if you can have it only to the right, start sewing at the top left of the zip). If you can, set the machine onto the 'needle down' setting, so the needle remains in the fabric when you stop sewing. Working on the right side of the fabric, begin from the top right-hand corner of the zip, about 6mm (¼in) from the centre seam. Sew down the long side of the zip, stop at the bottom, pivot the sewing on the needle and sew along the bottom of the zip, following the tacking line so you don't sew over

✂ **4**

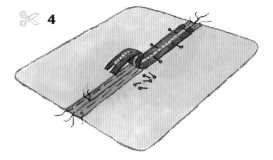

the teeth. Pivot again at the next corner, then sew up the other long side of the zip, pivot again, and come back to your starting point across the top of the zip. Clip the threads, pull through to the wrong side of the fabric and tie off. Remove the tacking and open the zip.

6 Take the bias binding and fold it around the piping cord. Ensure the cord is straight, but do not stretch it. Pin along the length of the binding, close to the cord. Machine-sew along the length of the binding, about 5mm from the cord, using a zipper foot.

7 Lay out the cushion back, right side up, with the zip running from top to bottom. Pin the covered piping around the edge, raw edges level, so that the two ends of the piping meet at the centre of the bottom edge of the cushion cover. Snip the bias binding up to the machine-stitching to allow the piping to lie flat around the corners (✂ 7).

8 Sew the ends of the cord together, trimming them if necessary, so they remain butted up, but don't overlap them. Trim the binding so one end overlaps the other by about 2cm (¾in). Fold one end under by 1cm (⅜in) and wrap it over the other. Tack the binding in place along the seam line (✂ 8).

9 Lay the cushion front, wrong side up, on to the back, checking that any motifs are the correct way up and the zip is open. Ensure all the raw edges are level, then pin, tack and machine around the seam line. Remove any visible tacking, then turn the cover right side out through the open zip. Press the cover carefully, avoiding the zip teeth if it is nylon. Insert the cushion pad and close the zip.

✂ **8**

✂ **7**

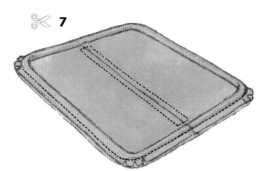

Customizing & Making Variations

You can make up the projects in this book by following the instructions exactly. But you may wish to branch out and make up a quilt that is a variation on one of the designs. Here is advice on how to do this.

Creating a different colourway

Always try out colour combinations before you buy your fabric and start to make up the quilt. Obtain small samples of fabric (you can often buy packs of postage-stamp-sized swatches from patchwork mail order companies), or buy the minimum quantities of the fabrics you are considering (usually 20cm or 25cm (6in or 9¾in) off the roll, or buy a ready-cut fat eighth).

Try the colours against each other, in the same ratios as they appear on the quilt. For example, if only a small amount of a colour appears on a quilt, your alternative colour should be represented only by a tiny piece in your samples. Take time to consider the combinations, and don't be afraid to try other colours.

One way of finding interesting colour combinations is simply to group fabrics randomly. If you have built an interesting stash or collection of fabrics, you can try taking out selections of fabrics at random and seeing how they look together. While this book is not intended to explain how to design your own quilts from scratch, this is a very good way to get inspiration should you ever wish to create your own designs.

When used together, patterned fabrics look best if they have something in common with each other, for example similar colours, patterns or scale. Although antique quilts may feature a jumble of all types of fabrics and still look good, this can be because the fabrics were printed using a narrow range of vegetable or early synthetic dyes. These fade, which adds to the harmonious effect.

Today's fabrics, with their wide spectrum of colours, can look mesy if indiscriminately juxtaposed. The most successful way to work with a colourful patterned fabric is to use it as the starting point for your colour scheme and match simpler patterns and plains to it.

Changing motifs

If you or your child has a preference for certain motifs, and these don't appear on the project, you can, of course, substitute or add them to the design. The Wild West Quilt on page 78, for example, is emblazoned with stars, but if you prefer, you could change these to hearts, or use a variety of simple motifs, such as hearts, stars, diamonds, circles, triangles, letters of the alphabet and so on. You can also add motifs or names to quilts.

A good way to check that you will be happy with the finished result is to make a scale drawing on squared paper first and colour in the shapes. A scale of 1cm to 10cm (1in to 10ins) works well for most quilts, but for smaller projects you may find 2cm to 10cm (2in to 10ins) is better.

Changing sizes

As bed and cot sizes vary quite considerably, it always makes sense to check before you start that the finished size of a project is appropriate. Do this by cutting, or by folding an old sheet and pinning it, to the correct size, and lay it on the bed or cot. Bear in mind that some quilts are just intended as 'toppers' – quilts that are meant to lie on top of the bed. Others are larger so they can be tucked in at the sides and foot of the bed.

If the given size is not suitable, you can easily scale the quilts up or down to fit different-sized cots or beds. If you wish to make a quilt larger or smaller, the easiest way is to adjust the size of the units. With a quilt made of squares, simply make these larger or smaller. To make a quilt 20 per cent larger, for example, simply enlarge each square by 20 per cent. Remember to make the border strips 20 per cent wider and longer too. It is not a good idea to make very large alterations to quilt designs in this way,

however, as the scale may begin to look wrong. Having very large or very small squares can also cause problems when you come to quilt the project.

If you wish to enlarge considerably a quilt based on a square unit, the best way is to enlarge the squares only by a small amount but add more squares. It is a good idea to plan this on squared paper first (see 'Changing motifs' opposite). However, if you wish to make a quilt smaller, just reduce the size of the individual squares instead, as reducing the number of squares can adversely affect the overall design of the quilt.

Suggested sizes for children's quilts

Pram/moses basket quilt
50 x 65cm (20 x 26in) to
55 x 70cm (22 x 28in)

Cot quilt
90 x 110cm (35 x 43in) to
120 x 200cm (47 x 79in)

Single bed
125 x 175cm (49 x 69in) to
150 x 240cm (59 x 95in)

Note
Conversions are approximate. Always check the size is appropriate for your needs before starting a project.

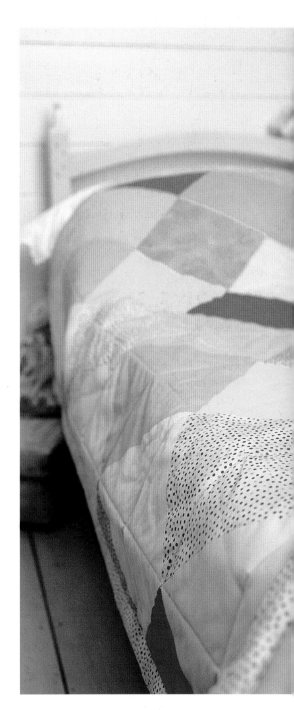

Templates

Some projects in this book require special shapes.
In this section you will find all the templates you need.

Accuracy is vital when making pieced patchwork. This means any templates you use must be drawn, cut out and used precisely.

You can buy ready-made templates of standard shapes in quilting shops, but it is quite simple to make your own. You will need card or plastic (see below) and a sharp craft knife, metal ruler and a self-healing cutting mat (see page 109).

Thick card is acceptable for making templates that will be used only once or twice. Old cereal packets are fine. You can cut window templates from card, which allow you to see the pattern on the fabric for fussy-cutting, in which case the card frame should be the exact width of the seam allowance. Paper is useful for very large pieced shapes and big appliqué templates.

Template plastic is firm clear acetate. Durable and accurate for continued use, its advantage is that you can see through it for fussy-cutting and you can easily trace designs onto it using a fine permanent marker pen. For speed and accuracy you can also buy template plastic with a grid printed on from quilt shops. Keep plastic templates away from a hot iron.

All the templates in this section are shown at 50 per cent of the actual size, unless otherwise stated.

Baby's Love Blanket

Springtime Baby Bag

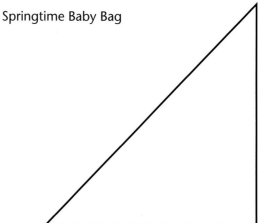

Patchwork Cat

Night-time Cushion

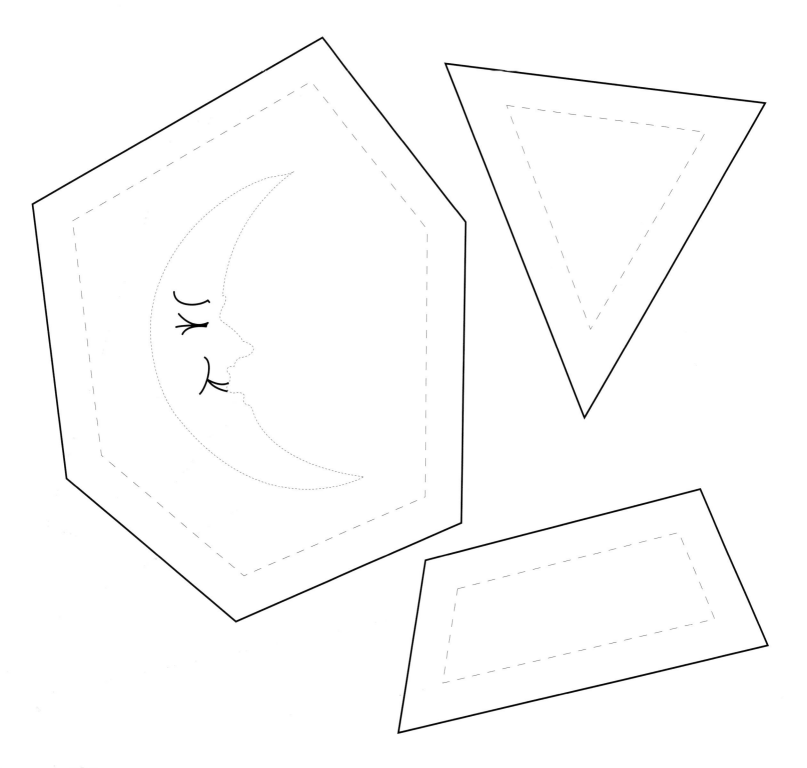

Windy-day Wall Hanging

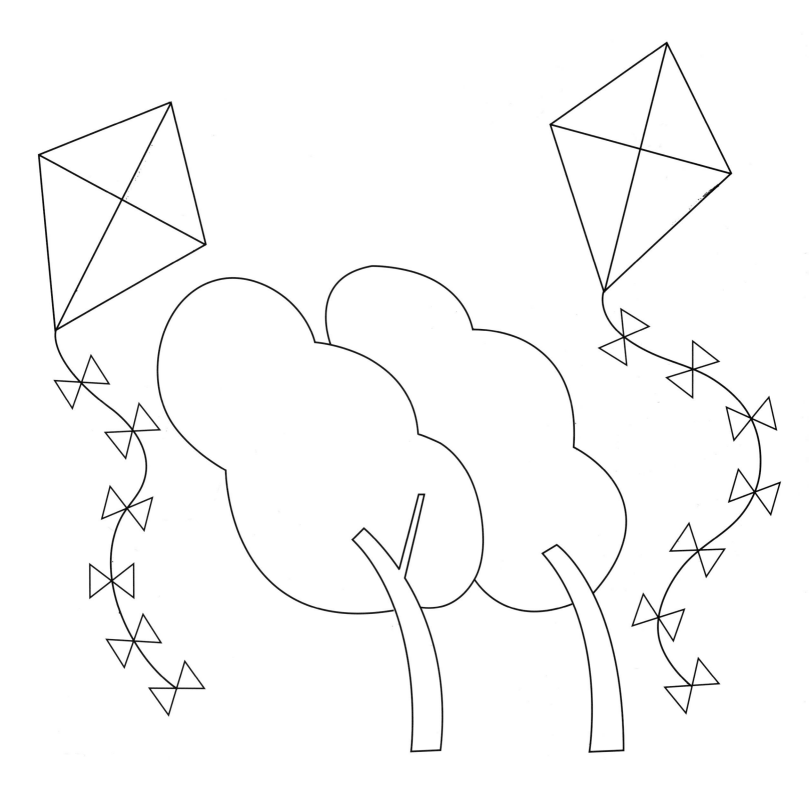

Alphabet Quilt

Sunny Sawtooth Quilt (100%)

Wild West Quilt

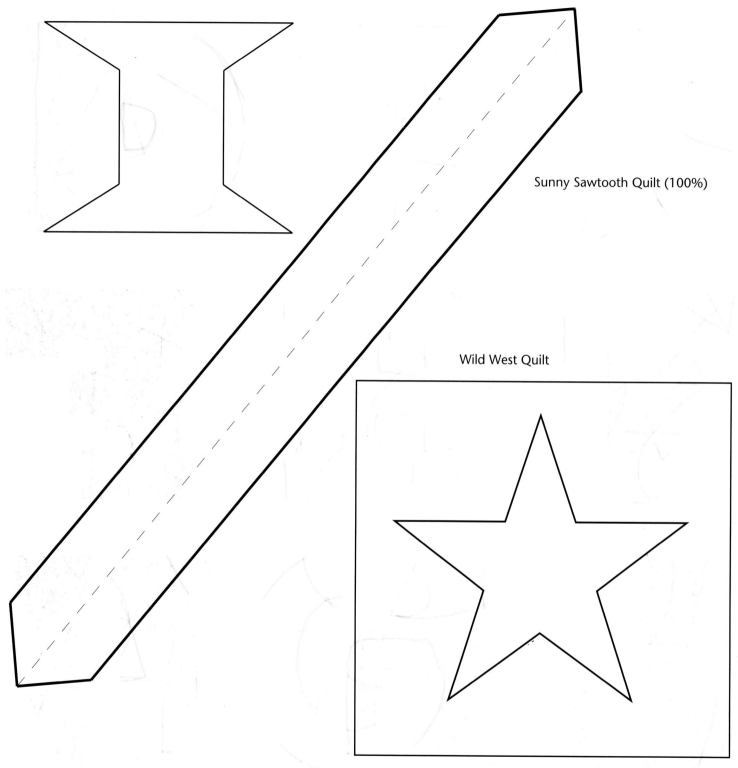

Alphabet Quilt

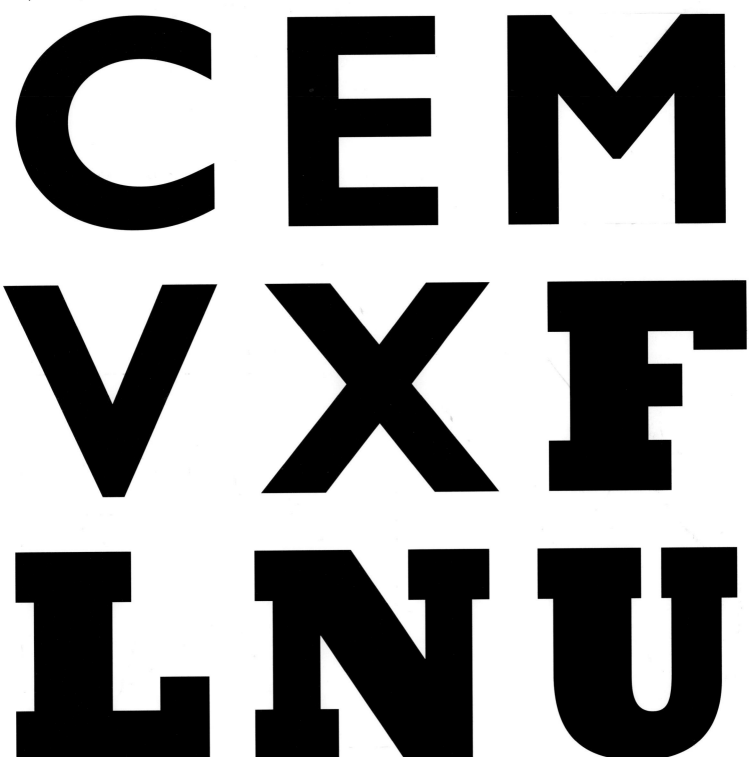

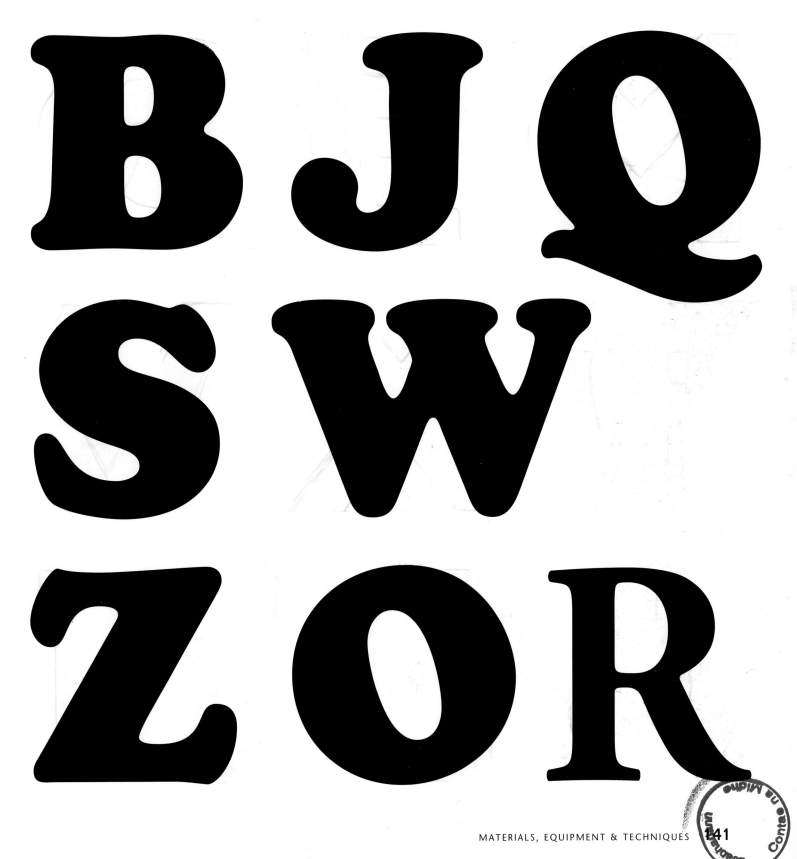

Index

A

age restrictions on projects 7
album (Friendship) quilt 82–5
all-in-one method of binding
  123
Alphabet Quilt 74–7, 123
appliqué 106, 118
  cutting out shapes for 119
  using satin stitch on 118

B

Baby Bag, Springtime 44–9, 132
Baby's Love Blanket 60–3
  template 132
backing fabric 111
  edges made from 123
backstitch 115
'bagging out' 120
basting spray 109
batting *see* wadding (batting)
bias binding 120, 121
binding a quilt 118, 120–3
  all-in-one method 123
  attaching the binding 122–3
  attaching a sleeve after
    binding 125
  bias binding 120, 121
  preparing the binding strips
    121
Busy Weekend 72–103
  Alphabet Quilt 74–7, 123
  Floral Quilt 94–9
  Friendship Quilt 82–5
  Night-time Cushion 90–3,
    134–5
  Sunny Sawtooth Quilt 86–9,
    138
  Wild West Quilt 78–81, 130,
    138
  Windy-day Wall Hanging
    100–3, 136–7
buttoning 17, 113

C

caring for quilts 127
Cat, Patchwork 50–3, 133
chaining (chain piercing) 111
chainstitch 115
chalk, tailor's 108–9
Checkers Sleepover Quilt 28–33
chevron stitch 116
clips, quilting 109, 113
colours
  cot quilts 41, 43
  creating a different colourway
    130
  polyester wadding 107
  thread 106–7
Comforter, Soft and Tufty 14–17
cot death 7
cot quilts
  Pink and Lavender 40–3
  suggested sizes for 131
  Turquoise and Maroon 43
  as wall hangings 124
cotton fabric 106
cotton wadding 107
Country Boy's Quilt 64–7
crazy patchwork 90
  and machine-embroidery 116
crewel stitch 116
cross-stitch 115
curtain hooks, hanging quilts
  from 124
curved quilting pins 112
cushions
  making cushion covers 128–9
  Night-time Cushion, template
    134–5
  Night-time Cushion 90–3
customizing quilt projects 130–1
cutting fabric 7
cutting mats, self-healing 108

D

designs, enlarging 119

diamond-in-square design 95
Diamonds, Powder-coloured
  18–21
double-sided adhesive webbing
  106

E

embroidery hoops 109
embroidery techniques 114–17
  embroidering simple and
    complex designs 119
  hand-embroidery 114
  machine-embroidery 116–17
  pressing embroidery 116
  stitches 115–16
equipment 108–9
  basting sprays 109
  embroidery hoops 109
  erasable markers 108
  light boxes 109, 119
  needles 108
  'O' weights 109, 111
  pins and pincushion 108
  quilting clips 109
  rotary cutters 109
  seam gauge 109
  seam ripper/unpicker 109
  self-healing cutting mats 108
  sewing machines 108
  squared paper 109
  tailor's chalk 108–9
  tape-maker 109
  thimbles 113
erasable markers 108

F

fabric 7, 106
  backing fabric 111, 123
  transferring designs to 119
feather stitch 117
finishing a quilt 120
Floral Quilt 94–9
Friendship Quilt 82–5

furnishing-weight fabric 55
fusible webbing 106, 118

H

hand washing quilts 127
hand-embroidery 114
hand-quilting 13, 112, 113
hand-sewing stitches 117–18
herringbone stitch 111, 117

I

interfacing 106
iron-on wadding 107
ironing, and erasable marks 108

J

joining patches 110

L

Laundry Bag, Undersea 22–5
Lazy Weekend 8–37
  Checkers Sleepover Quilt
    28–33
  Powder-coloured Diamonds
    18–21
  Quick and Easy Snuggle Quilt
    10–13
  Rainbow Quilt 34–7
  Soft and Tufty Comforter
    14–17
  Undersea Laundry Bag 22–7
light boxes 109, 119
Lively Weekend 38–71
  Baby's Love Blanket 60–3, 132
  Country Boy's Quilt 64–7
  'Me and Mine' Quilt 68–71
  Patchwork Cat 50–3, 133
  Pink and Lavender Cot Quilt
    40–3
  Safari Wall Pockets 54–9, 126
  Springtime Baby Bag 44–9,
    132
loops, hanging quilts using 126

M
machine-embroidery 116–17
  thread 107
machine-quilting 13, 112–13
markings, transferring 119
materials 106–7
  fusible webbing 106, 118
  interfacing 106
  quilt 'sandwich' 111
  thread 106–7
  see also fabric; wadding
    (batting)
'Me and Mine' Quilt 68–71
measurements 7
motifs, changing 130–1

N
needles 108
  hand-embroidery 114
  hand-quilting 113
  slip-hemming 118
  tying a quilt 113
Night-time Cushion 90–3
  template 134–5

O
'O' weights 109, 111
'on point' arrangement 18
outline stitch 116

P
paper, squared 109
patchwork 110–11
  Cat 50–3
    template 133
  chaining 111
  crazy 90, 116
  cushion covers 128–9
  cutting out shapes for 119
  joining 110
  joining rows 111
  Night-time Cushion 90–3
    template 134–5
pens, erasable markers 108
piercing see patchwork
pin-basting 112

Pink and Lavender Cot Quilt
  40–3
pins and pincushion 108
polyester wadding 107
Powder-coloured Diamonds
  18–21
pram quilts, suggested sizes for
  131
pressing embroidery 116

Q
Quick and Easy Snuggle Quilt
  10–13
quilt 'sandwich' 107, 111–12
quilting clips 109, 113
quilting machines 108
quilting thread 107, 112

R
Rainbow Quilt 34–7
rotary cutters 109
running stitch 115

S
Safari Wall Pockets 54–9, 126
safety notes 7
satin stitch 116
  using on appliqué 118
seam gauge 109
seam ripper/unpicker 109
self-healing cutting mats 108
sewing machines 108
  machine-embroidery 107,
    116–17
  machine-quilting 13, 112–13
  needles 108
  using satin stitch on appliqué
    118
SIDS (Sudden Infant Death
  Syndrome) 7
single bed quilts, suggested sizes
  for 131
size of quilts
  changing 131
  suggested sizes for children's
    quilts 131

Sleepover Quilt, Checkers 28–33
sleeves, attaching to quilts
  124–5
slip-hemming 118, 123
Snuggle Quilt, Quick and Easy
  10–13
Soft and Tufty Comforter 14–17
Springtime Baby Bag 44–9
  template 132
squared paper 109
squares, changing sizes of 131
squaring up designs 119
stem stitch 116
stitches
  embroidery 115–17
  for hand-quilting 113
  hand-sewing 117–18
  slip-hemming 118
  using satin stitch on appliqué
    118
stitching-in-the-ditch 112–13,
  123
storing quilts 127
Sunny Sawtooth Quilt 86–9
  template 138
swing-needle sewing machines
  108

T
tacking (basting) 107, 117
tailor's chalk 108–9
tape-maker 109
techniques 110–26
  appliqué 106, 118, 119
  'bagging out' 120
  binding 118, 120–3
  buttoning 17, 113
  caring for quilts 127
  converting a quilt into a wall
    hanging 124–6
  customizing and making
    variations 130–1
  embroidery 114–17
  finishing 120
  hand-quilting 13, 112, 113
  herringbone stitch 111, 117

machine-quilting 13, 112–13
making cushion covers 128–9
patchwork 110–11
quilt 'sandwich' 107, 111–12
slip-hemming 118, 123
tacking (basting) 107, 117
transferring designs 119
tying a quilt 113
templates 119, 132–8
thimbles 113
thread 106–7
  for hand-embroidery 114
  for machine-quilting 112
'topper' quilts 131
touch-and-close fastening,
  hanging quilts using 126
tying a quilt 15, 21, 113

U
Undersea Laundry Bag 22–5

W
wadding (batting) 107
  joining with herringbone
    stitch 117
  and the quilt 'sandwich'
    111–12
  tying a quilt 113
Wall Pockets, Safari 54–9
wall-hung quilts 124–6
  attaching a sleeve 124–5
  cleaning 127
  cotton wadding for 107
  hanging with loops 126
  using curtain hooks 124
  using touch-and-close
    fastening 126
  Windy-day Wall Hanging
    100–3, 136–7
washing quilts 127
Wild West Quilt 78–81, 130
  template 138
Windy-day Wall Hanging 100–3
  template 136–7

Acknowledgements

Author's acknowledgements
First, I would like to say a big thank you to my husband Kevin for being so enthusiastic about my quilts, for offering helpful criticism, and for putting up with months of chaos, upheaval and clutter in the house without complaint while I was working on this project. Equally, I would like to say a huge thank you to my daughter Isabelle for inspiring me with her unceasing creativity and enthusiasm, for being patient while I was working on this book, and for her beautiful drawings, some of which feature in these quilts.

Next, there are several companies to whom I am indebted for their assistance. I would like to extend very grateful thanks to Julie Gill at Coats Crafts UK for her unstinting helpfulness and generosity in supplying Coats and Prym quilting equipment and Anchor embroidery cottons. Thank you too to Vilene for their generosity in supplying all the wadding for the quilts in this book. I would also like to thank Zoffany for supplying fabrics from their delightful Caboodle Range, which are used in the projects on pages 10, 44, 54 and 78. Thanks too to Rowan for supplying fabrics from the inspirational Kaffe Fassett range; these are used in the projects on pages 14, 40, 50, 64 and 82. Thank you too to Zoe Phayre-Mudge of ZPM for supplying the fantastic novelty fabrics used in the project on page 40 and its alternative colourway.

Finally, I would like to thank the team at Hamlyn for being such fun to work with and their enthusiasm for this project. In particular I would like to thank Doreen Palamartschuck-Gillon who commissioned me, Sarah Tomley and Jessica Cowie who managed the project, and Anne Southgate who edited the text.

Publisher's acknowledgements
The publisher would like to thank following for the supply of items for photography **Cheeky Monkeys** for many wonderful toys. www.cheekymonkeys.com **Damask for the Home** for bedding, towels and children's night clothes. 3–4 Beoxholme House, New Kings Road, SW6 4AA Tel 020 7731 3553 www.damask.co.uk **Ecos Paints** for superb environmentally friendly paints. Unit 34 Heysham Business Park, Middleton Road, Lancashire, LA3 3PP Tel 01524 852371 www.ecospaints.com **The Holding Company** for a variety of boxes and baskets. Tel 020 8445 2888 www.theholdingcompany.co.uk **The Pier** for cushions, rugs and furniture. Tel 0845 6091234 www.pier.co.uk **The White Company** for bedding, towels, soft toys and childrens night cloths. Tel 087099555 www.thewhiteco.com

Photography **Octopus Publishing Group Limited**/Graham Atkins-Hughes 1, 2, 4-5, 6, 8, 14, 15, 16, 17, 18, 19, 21, 22, 23, 24, 27, 28, 29, 30, 33, 34, 35, 36, 38, 40, 41, 43, 44, 45, 49, 50, 51, 54, 55, 56, 60, 61, 64, 65, 66, 68, 69, 70, 72, 74, 75, 82, 83, 85, 86, 87, 89, 90, 91, 92, 100, 101, 103, 108, 110, 114, 120, 124, 125, 126, 128, 129, 130, 131/Dominic Blackmore 10, 11, 13, 78, 79, 94, 95, 98, 104, 106, 119, 123, 127

Executive Editor Sarah Tomley
Editor Jessica Cowie
Executive Art Editor Joanna MacGregor
Design Jane Forster
Illustration Kate Simunek
Production Controller Manjit Sihra

Stockist and Suppliers

UK

Coats Crafts UK
PO Box 22
Lingfield House
Lingfield Point
McMullen Road
Darlington
DL1 1YQ
Tel 01325 394237
www.coatscrafts.co.uk
Distributors of sewing and embroidery threads, and patch-work and quilting equipment, including rotary cutters, rulers and cutting boards.

Rowan
Green Lane Mill
Holmfirth
West Yorkshire
HD7 1RW
Tel 01484 681881
www.knitrowan.com
Distributors of Kaffe Fassett patchwork and quilting fabrics.

Stitch-in-Time
293 Sandycombe Rd
Kew, TW9
Tel 020 8948 8462
www.stitchintimeuk.com
Fabric and equipment shop.

Strawberry Fayre
Chagford
Devon
TQ13 8EN
Tel 01647 433250
www.strawberryfayre.co.uk
Quilting fabrics and supplies by mail order.

Vilene
Freudenberg Nonwovens LP
Lowfield Business Park
Elland
West Yorkshire
HX5 5DX
Tel 01422 327900
www.vilene.com
Manufacturers of wadding and non-woven interlinings.

Zoffany
Talbot House
17 Church Street
Rickmansworth
Hertfordshire
WD3 1DE
Tel 08708 300 350
www.zoffany.com
Manufacturers of furnishing fabrics.